IMPERIALISM AND BIBLICAL PROPHECY
750–500 BCE

IMPERIALISM AND BIBLICAL PROPHECY
750–500 BCE

David Aberbach

London and New York

First published 1993
by Routledge
11 New Fetter Lane, London EC4P 4EE

Simultaneously published in the USA and Canada
by Routledge
29 West 35th Street, New York, NY 10001

Typeset in Baskerville by
Selwood Systems, Midsomer Norton

Printed and bound in Great Britain by
Butler & Tanner, Frome and London

British Library Cataloguing in Publication Data

A catalogue record for this book is available from the British
Library

Library of Congress Cataloging in Publication Data

Aberbach, David
Imperialism and biblical prophecy, 750–500 BCE/David Aberbach.
p.   cm.
Includes bibliographical references and index.
1. Prophecy. 2. Hebrew poetry, Biblical–History and criticism.
3. Bible. O.T. Prophets–History of contemporary events.
4. Imperialism–Biblical teaching. 5. Bible. O.T. Prophets–
History of Biblical events. 6. Middle East–History–To 622.
7. Bible. O.T. Prophets–Language, style. I. Title.
BS1198.A24 1993
221.1'5–dc20   92-47228

ISBN 0–415–09500–X

לאבי מורי פרופ' משה אברבך

CONTENTS

List of illustrations	ix
Preface	x
Chronological table	xii
Map	xiv
INTRODUCTION	1
1 ASSYRIA AND THE FALL OF ISRAEL	19
Two Doom-Songs for Samaria	21
The Prostitution of Israel	23
Against Damascus	27
Song of a Vineyard	28
The Collapse of Israel	32
Tyre's Fate	34
Against Philistia	36
Dirge for Moab	36
Oracles on Arabia	38
Poems to Egypt and Ethiopia	39
The Fall of Babylon	43
The Warning	45
Isaiah's Poem to Sennacherib	47
The Restoration	50
2 BABYLONIA AND THE FALL OF JUDAH	53
The Age of Josiah's Reforms	54
The Fall of Nineveh	56
Songs of God's Injustice	59
The Battle of Carchemish	60
The Invasion	62
Nebuchadrezzar's Attack	63

CONTENTS

The Fate of Jehoiachin	65
Dirge for the Lions of Judah	66
Doom-Song for Egypt	68
Confessions of Jeremiah	70
Ezekiel: The Living Symbol	75
Lament for Judah	77
The Charge Against Edom	79
The Fall of Tyre	81
3 PERSIA AND JUDAH'S RESTORATION	87
Poems of Hope	87
The Fall of Babylon	90
Poem to Cyrus	93
Consolation	95
The Suffering Servant	99
The Stupidity of Idolatry	101
The Messiah	104
On the Warpath	105
The Day of Judgement	107
Bibliography	109
Index	114

ILLUSTRATIONS

All pictures reproduced by permission of the British Museum. © British Museum.

1 Tiglath Pileser III, probably during Assyrian invasion of Israel, *c.* 733–732 — 6
2 The siege of Lachish by Sennacherib, 701 — 9
3 Lion killed by Assyrian king, *c.* 645 — 15
4 Jehu, king of Israel, pays tribute to the Assyrian king — 19
5 Judean exiles from Lachish, 701 — 25
6 Assyrian attack on a river town, *c.* 865 — 30
7 Assyrian soldiers in pursuit of Arabs, *c.* 645 — 38
8 Nile sailing boat, *c.* 1800 — 41
9 Prisoners of war with Assyrian taskmaster, *c.* 700 — 49
10 Assyrian siege-engine in campaign in southern Iraq, *c.* 728 — 57
11 Scene of slaughter in Assyrian–Elamic wars, *c.* 663 — 61
12 Lion about to be killed, *c.* 645 — 67
13 Torture of Judean prisoners, Lachish, 701 — 79
14 Assyrian warship, probably built and manned by Phoenicians, *c.* 700 — 84
15 Demolition of a city in Assyrian–Elamic wars, *c.* 645 — 92
16 Ram-headed god of wood, Thebes, *c.* 1320 — 103
17 Assyrian king fighting lions, possible symbolic of his enemies, *c.* 645 — 105

PREFACE

This book has had a long germination and has been shaped by a number of people and experiences. Dr David Goldstein, late Keeper of Hebrew Books and Manuscripts in the British Library, first suggested to me in 1977, when I was a doctoral student at Oxford, that I try my hand at translating extracts from the prophets. For several years, working intermittently on these translations, I took part in a Hebrew Translation Workshop run by Dr Nicholas de Lange of Cambridge University. Many of the translations in this book were done with half an ear, as it were, for oral recitation in a relatively colloquial rhythmic style, this being close to the spirit of the Hebrew original – our habit of silent reading is, of course, relatively modern.

In the middle of this period, I finished my doctorate and spent two years (1980–2) as a trainee in child psychotherapy at the Tavistock Clinic. This training indirectly had a deep impact on my reading of the prophets. It stimulated much thought on the relationship between the inner life of the creative individual and external social and political reality. Translation led me to an increasing interest in the historical background of the Bible, and the prophets in particular. The frame of the present book, the last of several drafts, was determined by one observation: that each of the three surviving waves of prophecy appeared to coincide with a wave of imperial conquest in the Fertile Crescent.

This observation led me to sociology and religion and to a study of imperialism, including latterly a period as Academic Visitor in the Sociology Department of the London School of Economics, and the book in this way evolved from being an anthology of translations to an interpretation both of the relationship between political power and creativity and of the origins of Judaism.

The final draft of the book was written amid daily news of the collapse of the Soviet empire, when the Bible became the single bestselling book in the independent states. My feeling that the prophets were catching up with current events was increased when Iraq invaded Kuwait, precipitating the Gulf crisis of 1990–1. Iraq's dictator, Saddam Hussein, declared his aim of emulating the great Assyrian and Babylonian conquerors, particularly Nebuchadrezzar. More recently, the forced population transfer ('ethnic cleansing') of Bosnian Moslems by the Serbs is the latest of countless examples of a policy invented by the Assyrians and used against both Israel and Judah in the time of the prophets.

The poems entitled 'The Prostitution of Israel', 'Song of a Vineyard', 'The Fall of Nineveh', 'The Suffering Servant' and 'Confessions of Jeremiah' were first published in the *Jewish Chronicle Literary Supplement*. All illustrations are reproduced by permission of the British Museum. Special thanks are due to the staff of Western Asiatic Antiquities, the British Museum, for their patient help in choosing the illustrations.

I am most grateful to my editors at Routledge, Richard Stoneman, Heather McCallum, Sue Bilton and Maria Stasiak, for their invaluable help in the final stages.

This book will always be associated in my mind with especially happy memories of its inception and its conclusion: for it began life (though I did not know it) around the time I met my wife, Mimi, in Oxford over 15 years ago, and it reached its end at the time of the birth of our daughters, Gabriella and Shulamit. Indeed, the proofs arrived virtually together with Shulamit!

Finally, I thank my students at The Leo Baeck College, London, and McGill University, Montreal, with whom many of the ideas in this book were first explored, as well as a number of scholars, some of whom have asked to remain anonymous, who read the book, or parts of it, in draft form and commented on it: Professors Robert Alter, Fred Halliday, Dan Jacobson, John Sawyer and Michael Weitzman, and my father, my first teacher, Professor Moshe Aberbach, to whom this book is affectionately dedicated.

CHRONOLOGICAL TABLE

c. 745–727	Reign of Tiglath Pileser III. Assyria conquers most of the Fertile Crescent.
c. 740–700	Age of Isaiah. Hosea, Amos, Micah.
c. 734–732	War of Aram and Israel against Judah. Judah allies itself with Assyria. Israel is annexed by Assyria.
729	Assyria conquers Babylonia.
c. 727–722	Shalmaneser V is king of Assyria.
c. 725–697	Hezekiah is king of Judah.
c. 724–721	Israel revolts against Assyria.
721	Fall of Samaria, capital of Israel. End of kingdom of Israel. Exile of many of Israel's inhabitants to Mesopotamia. Judah survives as a vassal state of Assyria.
721–705	Sargon II is king of Assyria.
721–710	Babylonia, led by Merodach Baladan, revolts against Assyria and is defeated.
705–681	Sennacherib is king of Assyria.
701	Assyria crushes revolt involving Judah; besieges but does not capture Jerusalem.
c. 696–642	Manasseh is king of Judah.
681–669	Esarhaddon is king of Assyria.
669–*c.* 633	Ashurbanipal is king of Assyria.
c. 663	Assyria conquers Egypt.
c. 640–609	Josiah is king of Judah. Collapse of Assyrian empire.
c. 630–570	Age of Jeremiah and Ezekiel. Zephaniah, Nahum, Habakkuk, Joel (?), Obadiah.
612	Fall of Nineveh, Assyria's capital, and disappearance of Assyria. Babylonia takes over the Assyrian empire.
609	Battle at Megiddo between Judah and Egypt. Josiah is killed.

605	Battle of Carchemish. Egypt is defeated by Babylonia under generalship of Nebuchadrezzar. Judah becomes a vassal state of Babylonia.
605–562	Nebuchadrezzar is king of Babylonia.
c. 602–597	Judean revolt under Jehoiakim is defeated, Jerusalem is captured, and many of Judah's inhabitants are exiled to Babylonia.
c. 590–586	Judean-Egyptian revolt fails, Jerusalem is destroyed by Nebuchadrezzar, the Temple is burned down, and many more Judeans are exiled.
539	Conquest of Babylon, Babylonia's capital, by Cyrus, king of Persia. Persia takes over the Babylonian empire.
c. 539–516	Age of Second Isaiah. Haggai, Zechariah, Malachi.
538	Cyrus' Edict of Liberation allows exiled Judeans to return home.
c. 516	Consecration of Second Temple in Jerusalem.

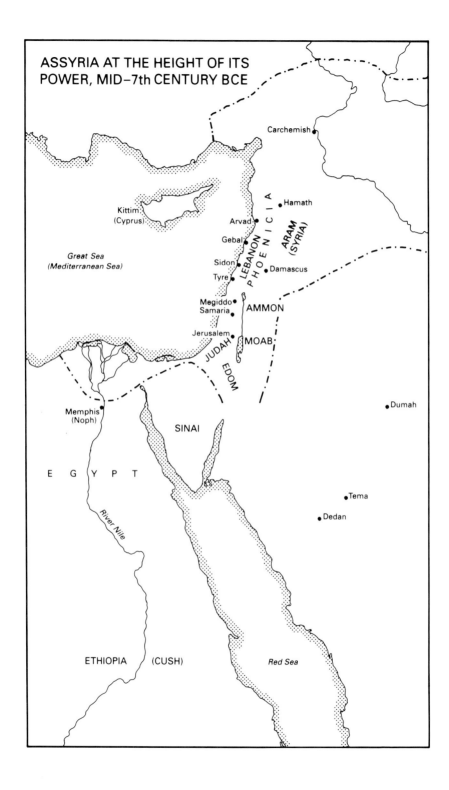

ASSYRIA AT THE HEIGHT OF ITS
POWER, MID–7th CENTURY BCE

Carchemish

Hamath

Kittim
(Cyprus)

Arvad

Gebal

LEBANON

PHOENICIA

ARAM
(SYRIA)

Great Sea
(Mediterranean Sea)

Sidon

Tyre

Damascus

Megiddo
Samaria

AMMON

Jerusalem

JUDAH

MOAB

EDOM

Dumah

Memphis
(Noph)

SINAI

E G Y P T

River Nile

Tema

Dedan

ETHIOPIA   (CUSH)

Red Sea

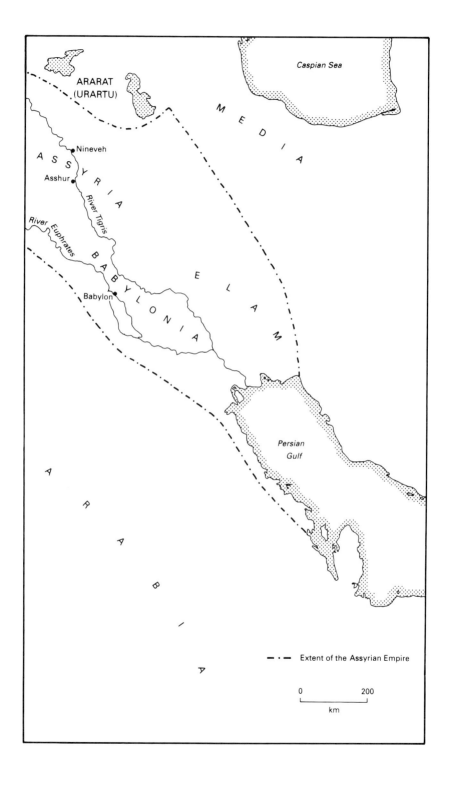

Caspian Sea

ARARAT
(URARTU)

M E D I A

ASSYRIA

● Nineveh

Asshur ●

River Tigris

River Euphrates

B A B Y L O N I A

● Babylon

E L A M

Persian
Gulf

A R A B I A

— · — Extent of the Assyrian Empire

0   200

km

INTRODUCTION

The poetry of the biblical prophets is inseparable from the empires which determined the history of the ancient Near East and the fate of Israel and Judah from the late eighth century to the end of the sixth century BCE* – first Assyria, then Babylonia and finally Persia. Each empire had its own character and motives and stimulated a distinct wave of prophecy, led by Isaiah ben Amoz during the Assyrian heyday, by Jeremiah and Ezekiel at the time of Babylonian supremacy and by Second Isaiah (the anonymous poetry appended to the book of Isaiah) during the rise of Persian hegemony. While prophecy was not confined to Israel, the phenomenon of prophetic poetry as it developed in Israel was unique and without a real parallel elsewhere.[1] It is one of the outstanding creative achievements in literary history and its impact on civilization is incalculable. It represents the triumph of the spiritual empire over the mortal empire; of the invisible God, king of the universe, over the human king of the civilized world; of losers over victors; of moral ideas over military force; and also, in a sense, of the creative imagination over historical facts. It is the only surviving body of poetry from the ancient Near East which, for the most part, belongs to a clearly defined historical period – though it aims in effect to extricate itself from history – 750–500 being the period marking the rise of the Assyrian empire until the restoration of the exiled Judeans to their land from Babylonia.

Although this poetry was written (or spoken) largely in response to the rise and fall of the Assyrian and Babylonian empires, it gives an extremely sketchy and misleading picture of the period. Judging from the prophets, Israel and Judah were central powers of the Fertile Crescent, equal in might and influence not just to the surrounding

* All dates referred to are BCE.

nations – Edom, Moab, Ammon, Philistia, Aram and Phoenicia – but also to the Mesopotamian nations which posed a constant threat. The fall of the kingdom of Israel around 720 and of Judah just over a century later did not occur because they were tiny, mostly insignificant pawns in the politics and economics of the region. Their defeats were not inevitable consequences of military weakness, of geographic vulnerability, of unavoidably inferior manpower and resources. They fell because of moral backsliding: had they retained their faith in God and observed the Law, the prophets imply, they would have been victorious.

Historically (though not theologically), this biblical picture distorts the facts, as archaeologists and biblical scholars have discovered in the past 150 years. Assyria, by the late eighth century, had built the most powerful empire in history to date, over a hundred times larger than Judah, with the vast majority of the population in the Near East under its rule. It had the strongest army ever to be assembled and pioneered revolutionary techniques of warfare, for example in the use of cavalry and the implements of siege – these would be used for the next two and a half millennia. Its success was owed not just to its military power but also to a highly effective bureaucracy based in Assyria, with a network of administration and trade stretching from the Persian Gulf to the Egyptian border (by 663 the Assyrians had conquered Egypt, thus gaining control of the entire Fertile Crescent). In addition, Mesopotamia had a sophisticated civilization, was a leader in many of the arts and sciences and had an elaborate polytheistic religion with a remarkable mythology, traces of which survive in the Bible, especially in the opening chapters of the book of Genesis.

The true character and might of Mesopotamia do not emerge in the prophets. Assyria and Babylonia (like Persia after them) are depicted at best as agents of God's will, commanded to punish Israel and Judah for their sins, and at worst as tyrants and idol-worshippers doomed to extinction. And this image of the ancient empires came down in history because the Bible survived while Assyria and Babylonia vanished virtually without a trace, their superb temples and palaces, their art and literature, their language, buried and obliterated. Whereas Jerusalem has been inhabited by Jews during most of its 3,000-year history from biblical times until the present, the great capitals of Mesopotamia – Asshur, Calah, Khorsabad, Nineveh, Babylon – were so completely forgotten that their very sites were for the most part unknown prior to the nineteenth century. While Hebrew was venerated and studied as the word of God, Akkadian, the cuneiform language of Mesopotamia, was lost for well over 1,500 years and deciphered only in the mid-nineteenth century.

If the Bible grossly misrepresents Mesopotamia, the hundreds of thousands of cuneiform tablets recovered in archaeological digs over the past 150 years yield little insight into the kingdoms of Israel and Judah.[2] These kingdoms are mentioned rarely, almost invariably as minor participants in extensive military campaigns or swallowed up in long lists of nations forced to pay tribute. While some biblical kings appear – Jehu, Ahaz and Hezekiah among them – no other biblical character, not even Isaiah ben Amoz or Jeremiah, has yet been identified in Mesopotamian writings. The destruction of the two kingdoms is given brief mention. The fact that they were, according to the Bible, a unique monotheistic enclave (albeit a flawed monotheism) in a polytheistic world is passed over in silence. The extraordinary characters and literature of the Bible left no known mark on Mesopotamian culture.

However, in their most brilliant creative achievements, Mesopotamian and Israelite cultures were not dissimilar: the toughness, violence and emotiveness of prophetic poetry have their visual counterpart in the magnificent wall reliefs of war scenes and lion hunts which hung in the palaces of the Assyrian kings. The prophets rarely condemn the Mesopotamian empires for their barbarity – for flaying their enemies alive, chaining them in cages, immuring them, cutting out their tongues and eyes, cutting off their genitals and feeding them to dogs, burning, impaling, piling up their heads or corpses, as depicted in their inscriptions. Violence and cruelty were part of the biblical world, and we may take passages from poems attributed to Moses and Deborah – both are described as prophets – to point out the violent thrust of biblical poetry. In the 'Song of Moses' (*Deuteronomy* 32), a bloodthirsty Yahweh thunders at his people for turning after strange gods of wood and stone, this being a frequent motif in prophetic invective:[3]

> ... fire burns in me, devouring
> the earth and its fruits, blasting the base
> of mountains, grasping out to hell –
> I'll heap misfortune on them, wasted with hunger,
> burnt-out by the plague of Meriri –
> fanged beasts I'll set on them, and maddened snakes.
> The sword will kill in the street ...
> As I live forever –
> I will make sharp my lightning sword!

I will make my arrows drunk
with the blood of captive and slain!
My flesh-devouring sword
on the heads of the wild-haired foe!

If these lines were spoken not by God but by an Assyrian conqueror –
Shalmaneser III or Sargon II, for example – they would be equally, if
not more, convincing as the outburst of a king believed to have the
authority of a god.

The 'Song of Deborah' (*Judges* 5), likewise, illustrates several features
of the prophetic style, particularly in the rhetoric, the repetition, the
imagery and the intense rhythmic excitement of Deborah's victory over
the Canaanites:

> The kings came and fought.
> The kings of Canaan fought in Ta'anach
> by the waters of Megiddo –
> no silver spoil for them!
> The heavens fought,
> the stars fought Sisera in their orbits,
> the river Kishon swept them away,
> ancient river, river Kishon ...

Here again, the triumphant mood is not unlike that in Assyrian art,
the Lachish reliefs for example, and also, occasionally, in the annals of
the kings. The touching vignette of Sisera's mother at the close of the
poem also recalls the Assyrian engravings of their enemies in defeat
and exile.

Each of the surviving three major waves of Hebrew prophecy came
about in wartime, and war is the subject of, or background to, most of
the prophetic poetry, even that depicting the golden age at the end of
days when swords are beaten into ploughshares and the wolf lies down
with the lamb: at that time Israel and Judah will gain resounding
victories over their enemies (*Isaiah* 11). Only then will God be 'king of
the whole earth' (*Zechariah* 14:9), an image of imperial rule deeply
influenced, no doubt, by the Mesopotamian kings who used an identical
phrase to describe the extent of their power (e.g. Pritchard, p. 297).[4]

Thus, by identifying itself with a spiritual empire, an immortal
kingdom of God mirroring and rivalling Mesopotamian kingdoms with
their feet of clay, Judah stretched the range of creative imagination and
in doing so held on to its unique identity even, and perhaps especially,
in exile.

4

While the prophets extol the virtues of submission, justice, kindness and mercy, their strongest moods are of angry defiance, accusation and bitter guilt; and this might be explained in the context of imperial expansion in the 200 years starting from the mid-eighth century. It cannot be accidental that the first extant written prophecies – of Isaiah ben Amoz, Hosea, Amos and Micah – coincide with an astounding series of Assyrian conquests in the second half of the eighth century. During that time, hardly a year passed without a military campaign. The cataclysmic effect of these wars of expansion may be gauged in Isaiah's impassioned prophecies to surrounding nations – Egypt, Ethiopia, Arabia, Aram, Edom, Moab, Phoenicia, Philistia, as well as Assyria and Babylonia. These prophecies barely acknowledge Assyria as the main cause of upheaval, perhaps because this was self-evident or as a slap at Assyria by attributing its victories not to its superior power but to God. The prophecies to the nations in Isaiah and later prophets, Jeremiah and Ezekiel particularly – there are about three dozen such prophecies in all – chart the course and impact of imperial expansion and give a unique outsider's view of the great events of the age. The threat of being overrun and the experience of vassaldom were among the most powerful spurs bringing about an explosion of creativity in Judah starting from the mid-eighth century. Prophecy served to control and make sense of otherwise uncontrollable, incomprehensible, earth-shaking events, to create something of permanent theological and aesthetic value in the face of impending disaster.

To explore the meaning of this simultaneous growth of empire and prophecy, it is useful first to outline the extent of the Assyrian conquests and to offer some interpretation of Assyrian imperialism in the light of modern theories.

Tiglath Pileser III, a general who usurped the throne around 745, was chiefly responsible for Assyria's rise as the first extended empire in history: he conquered most of the Fertile Crescent, made the northern and eastern borders safe from marauding tribes, and divided the territory into administrative units designed to protect the trade routes and to collect taxes with maximum ease. To these ends, he built a network of roads – the finest prior to the Romans – together with a chain of resting posts and forts. To ensure the disorientation of his defeated enemies, to make use of them and, finally, to assimilate them into Assyrian cities, he instituted a policy of deportation to the Mesopotamian heartland where the exiles were put to work on public building projects. As we shall see, this policy inadvertently had momentous consequences for civilization as it broke down ethnic barriers and

Figure 1   Tiglath Pileser III, probably during Assyrian invasion of Israel,
c. 733–732

opened the way for the future extension of prophetic influence and of
Judaism (and through Judaism, Hellenism and, later, Christianity and
Islam) as a universal religion. But at the time, deportation was a
catastrophe: Israel was exiled by the Assyrians and Judah by the
Babylonians, and this policy was reversed only by the Persians in the
late sixth century. The over-extension of the Assyrian empire, civil war
in the time of Ashurbanipal and the natural hatred engendered by a
tyrannical regime, weakened the empire. In the late seventh century it
collapsed and disappeared.

The phenomenon of Assyrian imperialism is crucial in the poetry of
the prophets. Why did the Assyrians build their empire? Why did it
fall, while Judah, for all its insignificance, survived? Interpretations of
imperialism have originated mostly since the late nineteenth century,
based upon studies of modern empires.[5] The word 'imperialism' was
originally used specifically to describe modern, not ancient, empires,
and there is a view among some scholars that it should be confined to
modern empires. However, scholars specializing in ancient Mesopotamian kingdoms agree almost unanimously that the word is applicable also to Assyria, Babylonia and Persia in the prophetic age,
inasmuch as the human forces underlying imperialism have not changed
greatly and its means and ends remain fundamentally the same.

Historical and theoretical evidence suggests that imperialism results from diverse factors: nationalism and economic pressure; the drive for power and prestige; greed, cruelty and raw energy; the struggle for security; and surprisingly, even humanitarianism and a desire to enlighten. Among these and other forces, the ones most obviously applicable to Mesopotamia are geography and economics, though religious motives are stressed in the ancient inscriptions ('The God Asshur, My Lord, commanded me to march ...'). Geographically, Assyria had no clearly-defined borders: it was surrounded on all sides by often hostile nations and tribes. While it had much fertile land by the Tigris and its tributaries, which attracted invaders, Assyria had few raw materials and had to import wood, stone, bronze, copper, wool, flax and, above all, iron. (This economic reality may have influenced the Mesopotamian worship of idols of wood and stone, which the prophets mock and condemn ceaselessly – such commodities, plentiful to the Judeans, were precious to the Assyrians.) A further destabilizing factor was the irregular rise and fall of the Tigris and Euphrates, which could lead to inadequate irrigation one year and flooding the next, and which required an elaborate and not always effective network of dykes and canals. These conditions forced Assyria to maintain a strong army and to look beyond its borders, especially to the Mediterranean coast, for raw materials. The eighth century was a time of expanding Mediterranean trade, and one of Tiglath Pileser III's chief military feats was the conquest of the east Mediterranean coast, with its trade routes and ports. His successors, Shalmaneser V, Sargon II, Sennacherib, Esarhaddon and Ashurbanipal, were largely successful in consolidating the empire and maintaining control over trade from Egypt to Persia and northwards to the Taurus mountains. The growth of international trade increased the strategic importance of Israel and Judah, straddling the land bridge between Asia and Africa, and for this reason the prophets were not entirely exaggerating in speaking of their land as central.

The picture of Assyria as the wolf come down on the sheep in the fold has blocked the impartial assessment of its campaigns for territorial expansion in the eighth century. To the sociologist Joseph A. Schumpeter, Assyrian imperialism was a sport, motivated by the basest instincts which are never entirely absent in modern imperialism (or, for that matter, in human nature) – bloodlust, greed, power-hunger, sadism and perverted sexuality: 'Foreign peoples were the favourite game and toward them the hunter's zeal assumed the forms of bitter national hatred and religious fanaticism. War and conquest were not means but ends. They were brutal, stark naked imperialism ...'[6]

Only in recent years, through evidence discovered in cuneiform, have scholars begun to regard Assyrian imperialism with any sympathy.

One historian, H.W. Saggs, has admitted that he actually likes the Assyrians and has suggested that, but for Assyria, Judah and Judaism might not have survived:

> Imperialism is not necessarily wrong: there are circumstances in which it may be both morally right and necessary. Such was the case in the Near East in the early first millennium. But for the Assyrian Empire the whole of the achievements of the previous 2000 years might have been lost in anarchy, as a host of tiny kingdoms (like Israel, Judah and Moab) played at war amongst themselves, or it might have been swamped under hordes of the savage peoples who were constantly attempting to push southwards from beyond the Caucasus.[7]

It is hard to see Tiglath Pileser III, Sargon II or Sennacherib as an unwitting saviour of Judah, but there is reason to believe that this was so. For in a sense, Assyrian imperialism forced upon Judah the discipline of monotheism and its teachers, the prophets. If left alone, Judah might have abandoned its faith and submitted to the paganism which dominated the Near East, making it far more vulnerable to assimilation and disappearance.

The discovery of the uses of iron – the greatest technological advance of the biblical era – made possible the type of imperialism created by Assyria as well as the defences against imperialism, the military ones and also, indirectly, the spiritual ones of the prophets. The Assyrians were the first to create a large iron weapons industry, and through the mass production of iron weapons put these instruments of destruction for the first time into the hands of sizeable armies. Iron changed forever the nature of warfare, travel and trade, all crucial to imperialism. The phenomenal Assyrian military successes of the late eighth century, news of which came to Europe via the Greek trading posts in the east Mediterranean, accelerated the growth of an iron-based urban economy in Europe, paving the way for the rise of the Greek and Roman empires. Assyrian improvements in the design of the bow, the quiver, the shield, body armour and the chariot (making it heavier, strengthening the wheels), as well as increasingly effective battering rams to penetrate siege walls and city gates, were largely made possible by iron tools and materials. Iron played its part in military training and combat techniques, in the building of roads and new means of rapid, flexible deployment of troops, logistics and administration. The poetry of the prophets echoes with iron: soldiers on the march, horses galloping, the glint of javelins, the thrust of swords, the clang of chariots.

While Assyria built the finest offensive army in history to date, Israel and Judah and other nations in the Near East developed some of the most sophisticated means of defence: walls, siege fortifications, gates, towers and protective structures on the walls, and engineering, notably Hezekiah's five-hundred-metre conduit hacked through the rock from the stream of Gihon into the city of Jerusalem.[8] Jerusalem was never conquered by the Assyrians, and Samaria, which in some places had walls thirty-three feet thick, resisted Assyrian siege for three years.

Figure 2 The siege of Lachish by Sennacherib, 701

The prophets were part of these defences, strengthening resolve against the moral 'breach in the wall' (*Isaiah* 30:13), depicting God as the only king and warrior-protector – 'shield', 'wall', 'bow-man', 'chariot-driver' as well as a type of smith-creator, removing impurities, battering the heart of his people into new shape, using the prophets as tools and fortifications. The prophet Jeremiah, for example, is chosen by God to be a 'bronze wall', an 'iron pillar' and a 'walled city' protecting the faithful (*Jeremiah* 1:18, 15:20). Significant, too, is other prophetic imagery of iron: the iron axe wielded by God in leading the Assyrians to victory over his faithless people (*Isaiah* 10:34), the iron yoke made by God to symbolize the supremacy of Nebuchadrezzar (*Jeremiah* 28:14), the iron pen to inscribe the sins of Judah (ibid. 17:1). At the same time, the prophets denigrate the uses of iron in war as in idol-worship, and the iron-smith is a target of the most vituperative mockery in Second Isaiah.

While Assyria's imperial growth stiffened Judah's will to survive, it also led to the destruction of Assyria within a century. The cruel force needed to build and sustain the empire aroused violent hatred throughout the Fertile Crescent; it died, as Napoleon put it, of indigestion. Demographically weak, Assyria could not hold down its huge empire. At virtually every opportunity, the subject nations, who provided much of the Assyrian military and administrative manpower, rebelled. Power was so centralized that the death of the king, who was believed to have divine authority, weakened the empire still further and often provided the best conditions for revolt. The seismic effects of the deaths of Assyrian kings are among the main events of the century preceding the annihilation of Assyria, and they decisively influenced the growth and character of prophetic poetry. After the death of Tiglath Pileser III in 727, Israel rebelled and was crushed and exiled. Against the background of revolt in the western provinces of the empire, Babylonia followed suit and waged a long and initially successful war against Assyria after the death of Shalmaneser V in 722. The death of Sargon in 705 led to widespread revolt in both the eastern and western sides of the empire. The death of Sennacherib in 689 again set off unrest which Assyria this time managed to contain rapidly. The death of Esarhaddon in 669 brought civil war and wars with Babylonia and Egypt. And finally, the death of Ashurbanipal in 627 triggered a massive revolt and the collapse and disappearance of Assyria.

The prophets' response to Assyria was inherently ambivalent. On the one hand, Assyria was hated and feared as the piratical empire that had crushed Israel and came within a hairbreadth of doing the same to Judah. This empire had an enviably attractive polytheistic culture, needing little or no military coercion to impose it on subject nations: the people of Israel, for example, seem to have assimilated willingly, though they had fought hard to keep their independence, and their kingdom and faith were lost in exile. On the other hand, if monotheistic faith was to survive, the Judeans had to learn to accept Assyrian victory as the will of God. This may be why no extended prophecies against Assyria are found in the period of its greatest military successes. Isaiah has no 'burden of Asshur', neither does Micah or Hosea; and the prophecies against the nations which start the book of Amos do not include Assyria. The vivid memory of Israel's exile challenged the prophets: how to maintain a monotheistic faith strong enough to keep alive a national-religious identity in exile as well as the hope of return. The lack of unity which had led to Israel's split into two kingdoms in the tenth century was another force which, paradoxically, helped Judah to survive. For after Israel's fall, Judah had over a century to ready itself psychologically for the possibility of exile, to avoid being swallowed up like Israel. The threat of exile concentrates a nation's mind wonderfully, and the prophets' writings are the full creative flowering of this concentration.

The prophets, then, were leaders in a war against cultural imperialism, and perhaps this was initially the main reason for the writing and preservation of their teachings. Though they accepted submission to the superior military power as a condition of survival, they subverted imperial rule in a number of ways: in their attacks on the materialism and injustice which were inevitable consequences of imperialism; in their apparent lack of concern with economic realities, which may be seen as a backhanded attack on the very foundation of Assyrian expansionism; in their insistence that the divine word was not the monopoly of priest and king in the sanctuary, but could inspire the common man, even a shepherd such as Amos; in their undying hope for the ingathering of exiles, which ran directly counter to Assyrian policy; in their readiness to admit defeat, to depict it graphically and to accept it as the will of God; in maintaining belief in one omnipotent God in opposition to what they saw as the paltry polytheism of Mesopotamia. 'The prophetic ideal', writes Yehezkel Kaufmann, 'was the kingdom of God, the kingdom of righteousness and justice. This was the basis of the first Isaiah's negation of war and of dominion acquired by warfare. This ideal implied the negation of world rule generally, of empire ...'[9] The unique ferocity of the prophets' attacks on idols and idol-worship, while largely ignoring the rich mythology of pagan beliefs, may have been less a sign of hatred for idol-worship *per se* than of the empires which were odiously identified with the false gods and the magic and superstition associated with them.

The late-eighth-century prophets were torn between detestation, hatred and fear of Assyria and identification with Assyria as the rod of God's wrath. Consequently, their hatred of Assyria was shunted to a large extent onto various targets: idols, idol-worshipping nations and Judeans who failed in moral self-discipline. But only with the fall of Assyria could this hatred burst out freely and without terror of reprisal. Loathing and fear of Assyrian tyranny are spelt out in the relish and glee with which the prophet Nahum depicts the fall of Nineveh and of the Assyrian empire.[10]

During the most stable period of the empire, from the middle of Sennacherib's rule until the death of Ashurbanipal, from about 700 to 627, there is no datable Hebrew prophecy. It is likely that Hebrew prophecy was suppressed, perhaps even by royal command, during this period. Manasseh, the Judean king for much of this time, reportedly spilt much blood, and the prophets might have been among his victims.

With the collapse of Assyria, Hebrew prophecy re-emerged and entered its second great period, against the background of Babylonian and Egyptian rivalry and the defeat and exile of Judah by the Babylonians. For a short time at the end of the seventh century, Judah seemed within reach of independence, but with the defeat of Josiah by Egypt in 609, it reverted to vassaldom. The motif of God's injustice – why do the righteous suffer and the wicked prosper? – emerges in prophetic poetry at this time, as if in response to the failure to gain independence at a time of the breaking of nations. The Babylonian defeat of Egypt at Carchemish in 605 was a watershed which left a strong mark upon prophetic poetry. With this victory, Babylonia took over the mantle of imperial conqueror left by Assyria. As in the previous century, Judah was caught up in the jockeying for power of Egypt and Mesopotamia, the prophets warning against alliances, especially with Egypt, which could lead to disaster. Jeremiah was jailed in besieged Jerusalem for his pro-Babylonian views and let go only after Nebuchadrezzar defeated Judah, burned down the Temple in Jerusalem and exiled most of its inhabitants.

Had the Babylonian empire survived for a century or two rather than a half-century, the Judean exiles might have assimilated into Babylonian society as the Israelites had in Assyria. The rise of the Persian empire saved Judah and, in effect, made possible the survival and growth of Judaism. Following his defeat of Babylon in 539, the Persian king Cyrus issued an edict allowing the Jews exiled by the Babylonians to go back to their homes in Judah. This act stimulated the third and final wave of biblical prophecy, dominated by Second Isaiah, which for the first time conveys the ecstasy of vindication, of having come through, the sheer relief of regaining the territorial homeland, and the gratitude to God and commitment to his Law.

The Jews, having survived, alone, as it turned out, among the peoples of the ancient world, felt an enormous sense of privilege, specialness, responsibility and chosenness. In the course of a single lifetime, the two most powerful empires in history, Assyria and Babylonia, had disappeared, while Judah miraculously held on. From the ecstatic viewpoint of Second Isaiah and his contemporaries, the earlier prophets such as Isaiah and Jeremiah had been proved right: faith in the end was indeed stronger than military force. And so, in their desperate search for defences against imperialism, the prophets discovered an alternative to empire which became the basis of Judaism in exile and, later, of Christianity and Islam. Faith is independent of time and place — this was their discovery — and they prepared the way for what Isaiah Berlin called 'a culture on wheels', a mobile culture built upon faith and viable in exile.

It is striking in the biblical account how the weakening of imperial rule both in the late eighth century and the late seventh century was accompanied by a turning back to Yahweh-worship and the destruction of idols, and how the discovery of the Book of the Law (believed to be *Deuteronomy*) occurred just when Assyria lost its military grip at the end of the seventh century. Most of the main elements of Judaism in exile appear to have crystallized into a religious way of life under Persian rule, at the tail-end of the prophetic period (the prophets vanished, one feels, because their task was done): belief in one invisible universal God and the total rejection of idols and magic; attachment to the memory of the Land of Israel; the introduction of synagogue worship as a substitute for Temple worship, and of prayer and study in place of the sacrifices; the repudiation of intermarriage; the invention of proselytization, this being almost a religious warfare equivalent to imperialism, and of the idea of martyrdom to defend the faith (as suggested in the book of *Daniel* which, although written much later, describes the Persian period), as well as the concept of the Messiah who would appear at the end of days and restore the Davidic kingdom of Judah. As indicated earlier, the exposure of the exiled Judeans to a kaleidoscopic group of other exiled peoples inclined them to develop their religion along far more universalistic lines than would have been possible in Judah. At the same time, the alienation and aggressiveness of some of the exiles gave rise to hatred, which was to develop into full-blown anti-Semitism during the Hellenistic period and onward.

The modern reader confronted with prophetic poetry for the first time might find it confused and bewildering in its fragmentation; unsettling in its violence, sentimentality and humourlessness; tendentious, arrogant, presumptuous and even mad in speaking in God's name; professing a universality which it does not necessarily have; a timebound phenomenon foisted on to later generations as an absolute, unchanging truth for all time. Yet if poetry is judged by its power to inspire, to change people's lives, their way of looking at things, Hebrew prophetic poetry is the most influential body of poetry in history. Every political and religious movement which stresses the value of social justice and compassion, opposes materialism and the unjust distribution of wealth, objects to ritual at the expense of spirituality and to the emphasis on the letter of the law rather than its spirit, and fights the abuse of power, owes something to the prophets. There is a view which extends prophetic influence even further: by freeing the world from magic, the prophets created the basis for modern science and technology and for capitalism.[11] However, from a creative standpoint the prophets' impact is most striking: all poets who write religious or political poetry, or in a rhetorical, confessional or lyrical mode are part of a tradition in which the prophets are among the prime movers, their taut, rhythmic, gritty Hebrew rich in imagery, contrasts and emotional range, of anger and tenderness, devastation and hope, vision and sarcasm.

The prophets, above all, helped transform Judaism from a national and parochial religion to a universal one, progenitor of Christianity and Islam. For all its bitterness, their poetry is remarkably hopeful and life-affirming, coming as it does from a people under constant threat of annihilation, whereas the outstanding Mesopotamian art is possessed by death. Death is the main subject of the finest poem of this civilization, the epic of Gilgamesh, which ends with Gilgamesh awaiting death by the magnificent city walls which he has built. Gilgamesh weeps to Urshanabi, the ferryman across the waters of death: 'O Urshanabi, was it for this that I toiled with my hands, is it for this that I have wrung out my heart's blood? For myself I have gained nothing . . .'[12] The most memorable representations in Assyrian art – the lions caged and trapped, pierced by arrows and spears, convulsed in dying agonies – may be taken in the end as a symbol of empire, violent and unloved, lacking spiritual direction, turning upon itself in a *Götterdämmerung* of despair.

The relevance of the prophets today lies not just in their religious and social message and their aesthetic attraction, but also in their condemnation of the greed and cruelty of imperialism and their creation of a spiritual alternative. This book aims, accordingly, to be an

Figure 3 Lion killed by Assyrian king, *c.* 645

interpretative history and anthology of prophetic poetry through each of the three major imperialistic periods – Assyrian, Babylonian and Persian. About three dozen outstanding poems and fragments are arranged in a running narrative starting from the late eighth century until the late sixth century. Though precise dating is rarely, if ever, conclusive and the authorship of many passages is in doubt – the nature of the problem may be appreciated by comparing *Isaiah* 2:1–4 and *Micah* 4:1–3 – prophetic poetry encourages a limited historical approach: the prophets often respond directly to specific events, and in many cases, such as Isaiah's poem to Sennacherib, Nahum on Nineveh's fall, Jeremiah on the battle of Carchemish, or Ezekiel's allegory on the lions of Judah, the dating of the poetry is fairly clear, and is often stated in superscriptions. (In some instances, Ezekiel gives the exact year, month and day of a particular vision, though he does not say how much time passed before it was written.) By reading in a loose chronological order these and other poems datable within a rough period (such as Isaiah's oracles to the nations), a vivid, idiosyncratic portrait emerges of the main events and changes in the Near East of the eighth to the sixth centuries.

The treatment of the prophetic books as anthologies of poems and fragments is justified by scholarly consensus. John Bright writes: 'The Book of Jeremiah, like most of the prophetic books, is a kind of anthology – or, to be more accurate, an anthology of anthologies –

15

and is to be read as such.'[13] To my knowledge, no such anthology of prophetic poetry has been done before. In fact, it is rare for these texts to be translated not by a committee or by authority of a committee, but above all as ancient poetry written or spoken in its time by men speaking to men and aiming at freshness, clarity, rhythm, power of expression and influence.

In any attempt to enter the world of the prophets, frustration in the end surpasses curiosity, the mystery overwhelms the sum of the facts. The poetry quivers with tantalizing questions, and it is well to conclude this introduction by giving an idea of our ignorance. So much has been written on the fifteen books of the literary prophets, which total just a few hundred pages in the Hebrew Bible – literally tens of thousands of books and editions – that one might think that a great deal is known. The opposite is true: so much has been written *because* so little is known. Our ignorance is betrayed in the following questions, a few among many which have no answer and are not likely ever to be answered fully: did the prophets visit Assyria or other countries which enter their poetry? Did they have any contact with other prophets in the Near East? Did any of them know Akkadian and, if so, how did this affect their prophecies? Did they write much that has been lost? Was there a written prophetic tradition prior to the age of Isaiah which has been lost? Did the 'false prophets' make written prophecies? If so, what was their literary merit and influence and what happened to them? Who were the audiences of the prophets and how widely were they and their message known? How did they live their daily lives? Were their prophecies ever set to music? How were their works edited? Who were the prophets?

NOTES

1 John Bright (ed. and tr.), *Jeremiah*, The Anchor Bible, vol. 21, Garden City, New York: Doubleday & Co., 1965, p. xix.
2 For a selection of some of the most important of these documents, see D. Winton Thomas (ed.), *Documents from Old Testament Times*, London: Thomas Nelson & Sons, 1958; and James B. Pritchard, *Ancient Near Eastern Texts Relating to the Old Testament*, 3rd edn, Princeton: Princeton University Press, 1969. Henceforth referred to as 'Thomas' and 'Pritchard' in the text.
3 Translations are by David Aberbach. Sources of poems translated are given after each poem and refer to chapter and verse of the Hebrew Bible.
4 'Amid the clamour of the multi-racial metropolis [Babylon in the sixth century BCE] the exiles must have watched the kings of many nations bring their tribute to Nebuchadrezzar and have envisaged the long-promised Day

when the same would be done not for a man but for their God as King of Kings in his new city.'
(D.J. Wiseman, *Nebuchadrezzar and Babylon*, Oxford: Oxford University Press, 1985, p. 115)

5 For bibliography on imperialism, see p. 113 below.
6 Joseph A. Schumpeter, *Imperialism and Social Classes*, tr. Heinz Norden, ed. Paul M. Sweezy, Oxford: Blackwell, 1951, p. 44.
7 H.W. Saggs, *Everyday Life in Babylonia and Assyria*, London: B.T. Batsford Ltd, New York: G.P. Putnam's Sons, 1965, p. 118.
8 See Yigael Yadin, *The Art of Warfare in Biblical Lands in the Light of Archaeological Study*, 2 vols, New York: McGraw-Hill, 1963.
9 Yehezkel Kaufmann, *History of the Religion of Israel*, vol. IV, *The Babylonian Captivity and Deutero-Isaiah*, tr. M. Greenberg, New York: Union of American Hebrew Congregations, 1970, p. 117.
10 See pp. 56–8 below.
11 Cf. Max Weber, *General Economic History*, tr. Frank H. Knight, New York: Collier Books, 1961 (first published 1923), p. 265.
12 *The Epic of Gilgamesh*, tr. N.K. Sanders, Harmondsworth: Penguin, 1960, p. 114.
13 Bright, *Jeremiah*, p. lxxix.

1

ASSYRIA AND THE FALL OF ISRAEL

Figure 4 Jehu, king of Israel, pays tribute to the Assyrian king

The above is the only extant contemporary picture of a biblical character. It appears on the mid-ninth-century Black Obelisk of Shalmaneser III: the Israelite king, Jehu (or his messenger), is on his knees with gifts of gold and silver for the 'Great Dragon', the Assyrian king (Pritchard, pp. 276, 281). This is the same wild, violent, heroic Jehu of *II Kings*, anointed dramatically by the prophet Elisha, assassin of the kings of Israel and Judah, of Jezebel and Ahab's seventy sons. Through Assyrian eyes, however, Jehu was nothing more than a cringing vassal. This image of prostration held true of Israel and Judah for the better part of the next two centuries, up to the fall of Nineveh in 612. Much of the political and prophetic activity in Israel and Judah during the century prior to the conquests of Tiglath Pileser III was in reaction to such humiliation and to further menace both from Assyria and Aram. The ninth-century Israelite alliance with Phoenicia, for example, was an attempt to form a military bloc to fend off mutual enemies. Likewise, Israel's peace with Judah, for the first time since the kingdom had split a century earlier, was precipitated by the threat from the north-east. At this time, too, the prophet Elijah, with Jehu's help, and his disciple Elisha did away with the Canaanite prophets and the Baal cult and established the Yahweh cult as the major religious force in Israel. The recognition that the God of Israel and Judah could not compete militarily with imperial might is implicit in Elijah's vision on Mount Sinai of the invisible God, speaking not with the fire and thunder of battle, but with the soundless voice of truth and justice.

Still, no written prophecies survived from the time of Elijah, and the Bible tells nothing of Assyria prior to the eighth century. Assyrian records show, however, that Aram and Israel fought a major battle against Assyria at Qarkar around 853 and apparently stopped the Assyrian army (Pritchard, pp. 276ff.). About a decade later, Aram attacked Israel and it seems that Jehu paid the Assyrians to halt the Arameans. During a brief period of Assyrian weakness, Aram overran much of Israel and Judah, but by the end of the ninth century Assyria recovered and fought a short, decisive war against Aram. With the defeat of Aram, the lost territories were regained and the military threat was temporarily lifted. The first half of the eighth century was a time of rare security and prosperity both for Israel and Judah.

The literary prophets, and the earliest firmly datable poetry in Hebrew, emerged at the end of this period of revival, when the Assyrians began the wars which led to their conquest of the Fertile Crescent by the end of the eighth century. The works of four prophets have survived from this time: Amos, Hosea, Isaiah and Micah. All, except probably Hosea, were Judeans and all, with the possible exception of Micah, were born in the time of relative peace and economic boom which had made Israel and Judah together as powerful as during David's heyday. By the time of their deaths, Judah was a vassal of the Assyrians and Israel was wiped off the map. The prophets were obsessed with the question of morality and retribution: if Yahweh was omnipotent and, indeed, the God of the nations as well as of Israel and Judah, how could he allow the fall of his people? They could admit only one answer: prosperity had led to social injustice and moral laxity. Israel was punished for its sins by the Assyrians, the rod of God's wrath, as Isaiah (10:5) describes them. And so, the prophets castigate Israel and Judah. Everywhere they saw moral decline leading to corruption and disaster. In the books of Amos and Isaiah, for example, the ignoble aristocrats of Israel (= Jacob) debauch themselves in the capital city of Samaria as military disaster threatened.

TWO DOOM-SONGS FOR SAMARIA

1

You alone have I known
among the families of men:
Therefore I will punish you for your sins!

Hoi!
Uncaring in Zion!
Safe on Samaria's mount!
Aristocrats ruling Israel!

Go to Calneh's ruins,
of Hamath Rabbah,
of Philistine Gath down south:
Are you better than they?
Is their border longer than yours?

You put off the bad day,
    bring violence closer.
You sprawl across your ivory beds.
You eat fresh lamb and calf.
You pluck the harpstrings,
Davids the lot of you!
drinking wine from bowls,
using the best oils!

You care nothing for your country's grief!

So − you'll be first into exile,
your stinking orgies will stop −

For I abhor Jacob's arrogance,
I hate his palaces.
I will cut this city off!
great house and small alike,
    smash to splinters −

Can horses run on rocks?
or oxen plough the sea?
But you − you've made justice poison,
and righteousness bitter fruit.

21

You're happy – for no reason:
'We muscled our way to power!'

Now I, Yahweh God of the Hosts, say:
I will raise against you,
House of Israel,
a nation to squeeze you
from Hamath up north
down to the plains of the Dead Sea!

Are you different from the Ethiopians,
children of Israel?
For though I took Israel from Egypt
I did the same for the Philistines from Cyprus
and Aram from Kir!

The eyes of the Lord
are fixed on the kingdom of sin:
I will annihilate it . . .

2

Hoi!
Arrogant crown of Israel's drunks,
fading wreath to its glorious beauty
which crowns the valley of fat –
its wine-stunned rulers!

Look!
The power of the Lord
will stream like hail, a killer-storm
flooding the earth with force.

The arrogant crown of Israel's drunks
will be crushed underfoot,
and the fading wreath of its glorious beauty
which crowns the valley of fat –
a fresh-ripe fig in late spring,
no sooner picked than gobbled up.

On that day the Lord of Hosts will be
the glorious crown, the crowning beauty
of his people, the survivors.
(from *Amos* 3, 6, 9; *Isaiah* 28:1–5)

The prophets' faith blinded them to the truth that Israel faced the best
military machine ever created and stood no chance against it. It seems
that they exaggerated the sins of Israel and Judah to explain their ruin.
(Job's comforters assume likewise that his sufferings are proof of sin.)
Yet, if moral decline had indeed set in, to what extent was this caused
or affected by the Assyrian threat? Could the abandonment of God
have signified that Israel felt itself abandoned by God? (Israel's turn
from Yahweh to foreign gods in its final years is seen in the Nimrud
Prism of Sargon II: on capturing Samaria, Sargon carried away 'the
gods in whom they trusted' (Thomas, p. 60).) Also, if Israel had been
firmer morally, would the military outcome have been different? These
are not questions which the prophets ask. Certain that Israel was evil,
they did not think of causes and motives. To them Israel had abandoned
her faithful husband and become a whore. The most powerful use of
this metaphor is made by Hosea, whose personal life intertwined with
his prophetic vision to become a national symbol. His marriage to a
prostitute who bore him three children – to whom he gave the symbolic
names of Jezreel, 'Not my People' and 'Unpitied' – is an ugly microcosm
of Yahweh's stormy 'marriage' to Israel, an adulteress punished by
divorce and exile. Yet Hosea's dark curses and violent condemnation
of Israel are mixed with rare tenderness, drawing upon metaphors of
wasteland and fruitfulness, and culminating in the picture of a baby
taught by its father to walk. Divine love triumphs over fury and brings
an effusion of hope for salvation and return.

THE PROSTITUTION OF ISRAEL

Share not, Israel,
  the joy of the nations!
You've gone a-whoring from your God,
on every granary floor
   loosed your love for hire ...

So the grain will fail them,
  the new wine play them false.
Back to Egypt Ephraim will be driven:
Up to Asshur, to lead a filthy life –
No longer live in Yahweh's land,
  nor offer wine to please him.
Their sacrifices burn for themselves alone,
  like the meat of mourners,

23

polluting those who eat it –
for they are not burnt in Yahweh's temple.

(What will you do on the holy days,
        the days of Yahweh's feast?)

        Look! How they go, fugitives,
plundered –
        Egypt will heap them up.
        Noph will bury them.
Their priceless silver will gather nettles.
Thorns will cover their tents

These are the days of reckoning,
these the days when scores are settled,
when Israel will know
            for its sins
which prophet was a fool
            and which was mad,
and why hatred has increased ...

'Yet, when I found Israel –
        it was like grapes in the desert.
Your fathers were like first-ripe fruit.
Then they bowed to Ba'al Peor,
        to the shame of Boshet.
They stank like the gods they loved.

Once Ephraim was firm as Tyre
        a palm by an oasis ...
Now he carries his sons to the slaughter!'

Give them, Lord ... what will you
give them?
            Give them
A womb that loses its babies,
        and shrivelled breasts ...

'I will drive them from my house!'
'I will not love them any more!'

Once Israel was a vine
        bursting with fruit:
As his fruit increased, so did his altars.
The better his land,

24

                the better his pillars –
Their love was split.
Now they bear the guilt.
Yahweh will break their altars,
knock down their pillars ...

'Ephraim is beaten
        his root dried up.
He will bear no fruit –
If they raise sons,
I will bereave them, every one!'

My God ... will turn his back on them.
They will be tramps among nations.

Figure 5 Judean exiles from Lachish, 701

'Yet – I taught Ephraim to walk,
        holding them by the arms.
They didn't know when I healed them.
I drew them to me with human bonds,
        the cords of love,
easing the yoke off their jaws,
feeding them with care ...

25

How can I give you up, Ephraim?
How can I make you like Admah and
Zeboim?
My heart burns with pity.
I will not follow my fury
    to ruin Ephraim,
for I am God, not man.
I am holy inside you.
I need not breach the city walls!'

Those who walk behind the Lord
    shall roar like a lion
    for he will roar:

'Let my sons come trembling
    from the river lands ...
Trembling like a bird from Egypt
    and a dove from Asshur –
I will return them to their homes!'

(from *Hosea* 9, 10, 11)

Under Tiglath Pileser III, the Assyrians went to war, defeating Urartu
in the north, subduing and annexing most of Aram, imposing vassal
status on western kingdoms in southern Anatolia, Phoenicia, Trans-
jordan and Philistia to the Egyptian border, and conquering Babylonia
which had rebelled in the south-east. Israel and Judah were affected
by this, the most extraordinary military feat in history to date, long
before they were overrun. There were swift, violent changes in Israel:
Zecharia, the last king of the Jehu dynasty, was murdered; his assassin,
Shallum, was killed a month later by Menahem; Menahem held the
Assyrians off by paying them tribute, but his son, Pekahiah, was
murdered by Pekah who, in turn, was struck down by Hoshea, the last,
ill-fated king of Israel.

  Anxiety at the Assyrian threat fills the prophecies of that time.
Around 734, Rezin, king of Aram, joined Pekah in a war against Judah
with the aim of forcing the reluctant Judeans to join a coalition against
Assyria. According to *II Kings* 16 and *II Chronicles* 28, Ahaz, king of
Judah, sacrificed his son (or children) as a burnt offering; some scholars
think that he committed this act to propitiate Yahweh in this crisis.
Ignoring Isaiah's advice, he turned to Assyria for help. Assyria, with an
eye on the trade routes along the eastern Mediterranean, was waiting
for just such a pretext to intervene. Ahaz accepted the yoke of
vassaldom, paying large tributes and adopting some of the cultic

practices of the Arameans. The Assyrians paid him by resuming their attack on Aram, easing the pressure on Judah. By 732, Aram was defeated and the Assyrians began their descent into Israel. Within a short time, Israel too was an Assyrian vassal. Isaiah minced no words in depicting the kingdoms of Aram and Israel, echoing Assyrian records in which their ruin is compared to a natural disaster such as a flood or storm (Pritchard, p. 283).

AGAINST DAMASCUS

Damascus is a city no longer
but a gutted ruin ...
Abandoned, the towns of Aroer
where sheep graze freely,
unafraid.

Ephraim will lose its fortresses,
Damascus its kingdom.

What's left of Aram –
like Israel shrunk,
says the Lord of Hosts.
             (*Isaiah* 17:1–3)

With Judah's submission to Assyria, biblical prophecy reached its high point in the poetry of Isaiah, a potent blend of hard moralizing and tender lyricism, of theology and aesthetics, history and universal truth. Like most, if not all, prophetic poetry, it is done in free verse, though one section (*Isaiah* 5, 9–10) is linked with a hammer-blow series of refrains. Its power is virtually a linguistic match for Assyria's military might, a rod of God's fury. Undercurrents of unease run through this poetry: for example, Judah's guilt at being an indirect party to Israel's subjugation through its alliance with Assyria, and its need to justify Israel's fall by denouncing the northern kingdom for abandoning Yahweh and his Law. There is palpable relief that Judah has not suffered the same fate – its position in hilly land off the coast and the trade routes made it less important and more defensible than Israel. Yet who was to say that Judah could avoid Israel's fate, seeing that it too was morally rotten. All that remained constant to Isaiah was in the empire of the heart – truth, faith, justice.

SONG OF A VINEYARD

A song of a vineyard
I sing to my beloved.

He had a vineyard
in a fat, brown patch.
He cleared the rocks,
    he dug the earth,
       he planted the freshest vines.
He built a fence, a tower, a cellar ...

He hoped to grow grapes,
but they turned out rotten.

Men of Jerusalem!
Citizens of Judah!
                Judge
Between me and my vineyard:
What more could I do for it?
I hoped to grow grapes.
Why did they turn out rotten?

Now I'll tell you what I will do to my vineyard:
I'll snatch its hedge for burning,
    smash its fence for trampling,
      lay it waste, unpruned, unhoed,
        strangled with briars and thorns;
And the clouds I'll command –
                      no rain for it!

For the vineyard of Yahweh Zebaot
Is the house of Israel. The men of Judah,
the joy of his planting.
He hoped justice would grow,
but there was bloodshed.
He hoped for righteousness,
but all that came up was a cry.

   The Lord let fly this word to Israel
that all the nation should know –
even Ephraim and the men of Shomron, who say
with puffed-up hearts:
'Though the bricks have fallen,

28

we'll build again with cut stone.
To replace felled sycamores, we'll plant cedars' –
that Yahweh will rouse Rezin's foes,
and stir Asshur to war –
Aram from the east, Philistines from the west,
to swallow Israel.

> *And still his anger burns,*
> *his hand stretched out.*

   Hoi!
Asshur, rod of my wrath!
My fury a stave in his fist!
I cast him at a deceitful nation
    to kill and to spoil,
      to stamp him like mud in the streets!
And still this nation won't repent
to the hammering God.
Yahweh Zebaot they seek not ...
Their leaders bring them to the jaws of ruin.
The Lord will have no joy in his young men,
nor pity his orphans and widows –
for the nation is wicked to the core,
fool's talk in the mouth of all ...

> *And still his anger burns,*
> *his hand stretched out.*

   Woe to those who make bad laws,
Who write injustice
to twist law from the poor,
rob them of their rights –
widows their prey, orphans their spoil!

What will you do on the day of judgement,
the ruin coming from a distance?
Where will you run for help?
Where will you hide your wealth?
     What will you do,
but crouch among the captives,
cower among the slain.

> *And still his anger burns,*
> *his hand stretched out.*

29

Figure 6 Assyrian attack on a river town, *c.* 865

Woe to those who call bad good
and good bad,
make darkness light
and the light dark,
make sweet bitter
and the bitter sweet!

Woe to those who think they're wise,
clever in their own eyes!

Woe to those who wake at dawn
to chase liquor, lingering after dark
for wine to inflame them!

Who feast on the harp, the psaltery,
the tabret and flute,
and wine.

   Hoi!
Valorous drinkers!
Drunk – with the bribes of the wicked,
cheating good men of justice!

So, they will be as straw to fire.
Their root will turn rotten.
Their flower will turn to dust.
They loathed the law of Yahweh Zebaot,
cursed the word of Kedosh Yisrael.
This is why Yahweh is angry with his people.
He stretched out his hand and struck.
The hills shook.
Corpses fill the streets like dung.

> *And still his anger burns,*
> *his hand stretched out?*

(from *Isaiah* 5, 9, 10, 11)

The compensatory element of prophetic poetry is especially clear in Isaiah: Judah was weak militarily, but in the empire of faith it had the power of supreme rule. Yet for all its rhetorical force, this poetry has human frailty for its theme. Against the background of Assyria's drive southward, Yahweh is depicted as a cuckolded husband or a disappointed father, betrayed and uncomprehending, full of lust for revenge. In this crisis, the prophets hark back to the idealized early years of Yahweh's 'marriage' to Israel and to the happy 'childhood' of the nation. The importance of this mythologized history seems to have grown in proportion to the severity of the military threat. The prophets tried, in effect, to buttress crumbling national identity by asserting what seemed, in their view, firm, unchanging and unique in the Israelite tradition.

Micah, for example, affirms the wilderness bond between Yahweh and Israel. He sums up the essential moral principles on which the bond is based. The chaos and injustice of the present, he declares, might be undone by taking Israel's 'case' to the most powerful symbols of permanence and order – the mountains. The mountains will confirm the endurance of Yahweh's covenant, and the justice preserving it.

Perhaps only a nation like Judah, frequently under severe political and military pressure, could produce holy men and poets with so fine-tuned a sense of justice as Micah. To some later prophets, such as Ezekiel and Haggai, Temple ritual was of primary importance. But in general, the prophets emphasize moral principles and qualities of character, rather than power and the trappings of faith such as sacrifices. Yahweh's demands are stated succinctly at the end of the following poem in the book of Micah.

THE COLLAPSE OF ISRAEL

Allelai!
No good men are left!
Each hunts the other, with nets.
Son abuses father,
daughter her mother and mother-in-law ...

Man's foes – his own family!

Hear – you mountains!
firm, rocky foundations of the earth:
Decide
Yahweh's quarrel with his people ...

My people! What have I done
to make you weary of me?
Answer!

I freed you from slavery in Egypt!
I sent Moses, Aaron and Miriam ...
My people! Remember
the king of Moab, Balak's plot – and the speech
of Balaam ben Peor – then, from Shittim to Gilgal,
the crossing into the land of Israel!
Remember the acts of Yahweh!

And if you ask:
How shall I come to Yahweh
and bow to him?

Shall I come with burnt-offerings,
with year-old calves?

Will God want rams by the thousand,
and rivers of oil?

Shall I sacrifice my first-born son
to atone for my sin?

Man – he's told you what is good!
What does Yahweh want of you?
Only to do justice,
to love kindness,
to go humbly with your God ...

(from *Micah* 6, 7)

Justice, kindness, modesty – words which may have had a bitterly ironic ring under Assyrian rule – might also have been used as code-words for revolt. No prophet seems to have called for armed revolt, knowing it to be futile. Yet the moral principles of Yahweh-worship, as well as many of the rituals and customs of the Israelites, were unlike those of Assyria and went side by side with political independence. Religious suppression, even if it appeared to be voluntary, was a psychological part of their political servitude. The submission of Israel and Judah to imperial power seems always to have been forced by necessity, and at virtually every sign of serious weakness in the empire, they rebelled. As we have seen, following the death of Tiglath Pileser III in 727, Israel revolted but was defeated, and after a siege of three years, Samaria fell in 721. A large number of the Israelites were deported to northern Mesopotamia and to Media beyond the Tigris river, where their national identity faded. Israel thus became an Assyrian province, renamed Samaria, and was repopulated with Babylonians, Arameans and others.

The Judean prophets' fierce insistence on purity in faith was linked to Israel's annihilation. For apart from its land, all that Judah had that was uniquely its own, generating unity, purpose and the potential for survival, was its faith. Weak faith was equal to weak national identity. With the loss of faith, the ten tribes of Israel lost their land and identity, and the prophets raged at their surviving people like a father trying to protect his endangered child.

Judah did not take part in Israel's revolt and was spared deportation. The Judeans paid for survival with tribute and assimilation; shadowed by Israel's fate, they had little choice but to submit to the Assyrians, though it is not clear whether or to what extent Ahaz's adoption of pagan customs was forced or voluntary.

In the next few years, however, Assyria tired itself with campaigns against Phoenicia, Aram, Egypt, Elam, and most important of all, briefly lost control of Babylonia in a revolt led by Merodach Baladan

(721–710). Many, if not all, the prophecies in *Isaiah* to the nations are responses to these wars, which went on annually during the rule of Sargon II. These prophecies – such as the ones on Tyre, Philistia, Moab, Arabia, Ethiopia, Egypt and Babylon – give a clear picture of the scope of Assyrian conquests and their impact on the Near East. In fact, though, Assyria is rarely mentioned by name: instead, the upheavals are ascribed to a northern power, an anonymous plunderer, a sword and bow, a hard master, or directly to God. The subjugation of Tyre, for example, was one of Assyria's key victories, for it gave Assyria control over a vital link in the Mediterranean trade routes. It also enhanced Assyria's prestige as the military superpower of its time: Tyre's location on a rock island off the coast made it almost impregnable, but it was forced to submit and to pay tribute. This and other victories also consolidated Assyria's status as the richest nation in the world, and the fruits of this victory appeared in the magnificent capitals of Khorsabad and Nineveh built within the next three decades. Yet Isaiah ascribes Tyre's fall not to the Assyrian army but to God. The terse *envoi* is a sketch of Tyre seventy years later – a once-forgotten whore restored to wealth and power.

TYRE'S FATE

Howl! ships of Tarshish
for your homes are plundered!

Dumbstruck is Cyprus
and the Mediterranean coast,
once full of Zidon's merchants,
trading in Egyptian grain,
harvest of the Nile –
for Tyre was market of nations ...

Despair, Zidon! for the sea-fortress said:
I was never in labour,
I never gave birth,
I never raised
your young men and women ...

The news will terrify Egypt.

Howl! men of Tyre:
Take refuge in Tarshish!

Is this your good-time town of old,
settling foreign lands?

Who brought this on Tyre,
    Phoenicia's crown,
whose traders were princes,
salt of the earth?

God of Hosts has done this
to pierce their pride,
to mock these honourable men.

Pour from your land like the Nile,
people of Tarshish: your harbour is gone,
nothing holds you there.

God has struck the sea,
shaken kingdoms, commanded the ruin
of Canaan's fortresses.

*Howl! ships of Tarshish
for your homes are plundered!*

Envoi: Whore's Song

        take harp
        circle city
        forgotten whore
        play well
        sing much
        be remembered
            (*Isaiah* 23:1–11, 14, 16)

Another vital link in the chain of nations on the eastern side of the
Fertile Crescent was Philistia, in the coastal lowlands west and south-
west of Judah. In the confusion of the war waged against Judah by
Israel and Aram (734–732), the Philistines (like the Edomites) had
invaded Judean territory, and gave Ahaz a further motive for seeking
Assyrian protection. Unlike Judah, which paid the Assyrians tribute,
the Philistines tried to resist Assyrian rule and were overrun. As a
longtime enemy of Philistia as well as a subject state of Assyria, Judah
was hated by the Philistines, and Ahaz's death (*c.* 720) set off rejoicing

in Philistia. Isaiah's poem, which dates from the year of Ahaz's death, is a warning of Philistia's impending doom and an assertion of Judah's God-given power.

AGAINST PHILISTIA

Rejoice not, Philistia,
that the enemy-king is dead –
broken the rod that broke you –
for the snake will breed a viper,
its seed – a flying serpent.

While the poor earn their bread,
sleep safe, lamb-like,
your nobles I will starve.
The rest will be killed.

Howl, gate!
                Cry, city!

Philistia, melt away,
for a smoke-cloud gathers
from the north ...

And what shall be said
to the messengers of the nations?
That God has made Zion strong!
There the poor will shelter ...
                (*Isaiah* 14:29–32)

Judah's relations with Moab, to the west, were better than those with Philistia and, judging from the only surviving relic of the Moabite language, on the Moabite Stone (discovered in 1868), Moab had a language and, presumably, a culture very similar to Judah's (Thomas, pp. 195ff.). Moab's defeat by Assyria called up the following dirge by Isaiah in which criticism of the arrogance traditionally attributed to Moab is offset by poignant empathy, which may have been roused by Moabite refugees in Judah.

DIRGE FOR MOAB

Send a messenger to Judah's king
from the desert-crags to Mount Zion –

for the Moabites flee like scattered birds
to the Arnon crossing:

'Tell us what to do!
Make us a plan! Hide us!
Don't give us away!
Give our exiles a home!
Protect Moab from the plunderer!
for Judah is rid of plunder and extortion,
its oppressor is gone!
And Judah's throne is built on mercy,
its king rules by truth,
seeks justice – acts quickly!'

         *   *   *

We have heard of Moab's pride,
its overweening pride,
its wrath and lies –

So Moab will bewail itself,
every part of it –
for the grapes of Kir-hareseth,
bitter grief . . .

the vines of Heshbon are faded
and the vines of Sibmah,
intoxicator of kings,
whose tendrils stretched over the border
to Ya'azer, wandered through the desert
across the Dead Sea.

Therefore I weep
the tears of Ya'azer,
the vines of Sibmah,
weep bitterly for Heshbon and Elaleh,
for the battle cry
has ended your harvest . . .

                         (*Isaiah* 16:1–9)

Other poems of Isaiah's to the nations include one to Arabia, also
subjugated by Assyria, and the mysterious oracle to Dumah, which is
both the name of a place in the Arabian peninsula and the Hebrew
word for silence.

ORACLES ON ARABIA

Sleep in the wilds of Arabia,
fugitive caravans of Dedan!

Give water to these thirsty men!

The Temites brought them bread,
these men who fled the sword,
the outdrawn sword, the outstretched bow,
fled the heavy war . . .

Figure 7 Assyrian soldiers in pursuit of Arabs, *c.* 645

An oracle of silence:
A voice calls me from Seir:
Watchman, how far to dawn?
Watchman!
How far to dawn?

The watchman said:
Dawn comes, night too:
If you want, ask −
come back,
come . . .

(*Isaiah* 21:13–15, 11–12)

Assyria's two main enemies, Egypt and Babylonia, lying at opposite
ends of the Fertile Crescent, were the greatest prizes in its wars, and
the control of these farflung territories tested Assyria's imperial power

and cohesion. Egypt, being further away, was the harder military and administrative challenge. Eventually, however, it was subdued, though not yet defeated, by Sargon II, who transferred an Assyrian population to Egypt and forced Egypt to trade with Assyria. Egypt's attempts to stave off the Assyrians through magic are depicted graphically in *Isaiah*. Again, the Assyrians go unmentioned and the true author of these momentous events is Yahweh.

POEMS TO EGYPT AND ETHIOPIA

Here comes Yahweh on a cloud
swiftly riding into Egypt,
whose idols will shudder,
whose heart will melt –

I will set Egypt against Egypt,
brother will fight brother,
city against city, kingdom against kingdom:
Egypt's spirit will be punctured,
They will go to idols,
    to spirits of the dead,
to sorcerers and necromancers . . .

But I will turn Egypt over
    to hard masters.
A cruel king will rule them,
says the Lord God of Hosts!

The Nile delta will go dry,
    the river too,
boat and fish will vanish,
the arms of the Nile will sink and shrivel,
rush and reed will wither.
The naked Nile and banks of the Nile
will dry up, pass away and be no more.

The fishermen will mourn,
and all who cast hook and net on the waters,
the flaxcombers and cottonweavers
will shrivel in shame,
and the dam-builders for the fishponds
will be crushed in misery.

Fools – princes of Tanis.
Pharaoh's best advisers – bad advice:
How can you say to Pharaoh,
'I come from a line of wise men,
        a scion of ancient kings!'

Where are the wise men?
Let them tell you the Lord of Hosts'
        advice to Egypt:

The princes of Tanis are fools,
The princes of Noph are fooled.
Egypt's tribal leaders lead him nowhere.

God has mixed them up.
They will get Egypt totally lost
        as a drunk is lost in his vomit
and nothing will be done ...

                    *   *   *

    Hoi!
Land of winged echoes
beyond the rivers of Ethiopia,
whose messengers ride in papyrus boats!

Go back, swift riders,
to your tall bronzed people,
warriors feared in distant parts,
to your river-split land.

Tell them this:
To all who live on this earth –
When the war-banner rises over the hills,
        you will see it!
When the trumpet sounds –
                    you will hear it!

For the Lord said this to me:
As on a clear day in harvest heat,
when the raincloud passes,

Figure 8   Nile sailing boat, *c.* 1800

blossoms fall, fruit ripens,
and the twigs and shoots are pruned ...
I will watch in silence from Jerusalem:

They will be summer food for vultures,
winter food for wild beasts −

Then the tall bronzed people
feared in distant parts, warriors
of the river-split land
will bring gifts to God of Hosts,
to his temple on Mount Zion ...

(*Isaiah* 19:1−14; 18)

The most important events of the age – though one would hardly guess this from the prophets – took place north-east of Israel as Assyria and Babylonia fought for dominance. These kingdoms had the same Akkadian language and polytheistic culture and were not unlike Israel and Judah, frequently at odds with each other, one (Assyria, Israel) the more militant, the other (Babylonia, Judah) a leader in religious culture. Tiglath Pileser III had conquered Babylonia in 729, shortly after his subjugation of Israel, and made himself king of Babylonia. When Sargon II became king in 721, Babylonia revolted and, after initial success, was defeated, and the same happened when Sennacherib came to the throne in 705. When Elam intervened against the Assyrians, Sennacherib made a display of Assyrian power by razing the capital city Babylon in 689 and then flooding it.

A number of prophecies against Babylon have survived in *Isaiah*, though in no case is the dating certain. It is thought by some scholars that Isaiah's great dirge for Babylon ('How was the tyrant stopped') might originally have been addressed by an anonymous prophet against Assyria at the time of its fall in the late seventh century, but later was altered and inserted among Isaiah's oracles to the nations, which include an authentic prophecy on Babylon ('Fallen, fallen, is Babylon'). The reader who doubts that such displacements are possible should compare two identical prophecies in *Jeremiah* (49:19–20; 50:44–5), the first directed against Edom and Tema and the second against Babylonia. The absence in *Isaiah* of any extended prophecy against Assyria is strange, though there are some uncomplimentary allusions to Assyria (7:20, 10:12ff., 14:25, 31:8). Also, the Assyrian kings often designated themselves kings of Babylon, so the prophecies against Babylonia might, in fact, have been directed against Assyria. Still, there are reasons for thinking that Isaiah's dirge for Babylon was not originally aimed at Assyria. For Isaiah apparently saw Assyria primarily as the agent of God's will and, so far as we know, until the Assyrian siege of Jerusalem in 701, he called for appeasement, not resistance. In one extraordinary passage (19:23–5, which some scholars, however, regard as a later interpolation), he envisaged Assyria with Egypt and Israel as a triumvirate living together in peace and prosperity. To the Judean prophet, Babylonia's defeats in 729, 710 and 703 were the execution of the will of God, though the fall of the tyrant could also implicitly be seen as a harbinger of the fall of other tyrants – including Assyria.

THE FALL OF BABYLON

1

Terror grips me, and confusion,
this lovely evening turned to nightmare ...
Table set, lamps lit, feasting, drinking –
Then –

Up princes! Oil your shield!

For the Lord had told me this:
Act as a watchman, speak out what you see!

A chariot I saw, a team of horses,
    donkey and rider, camel and rider.
I strained to hear their message,
and I roared:

Fallen, fallen is Babylon.
all her idols smashed
to earth!

O Israel, thrashed and scattered:
I tell you this
which I heard from the Lord of Hosts
God of Israel!

2

How was the tyrant stopped!
How did the torture stop!

God has broken the tyrant's rod,
sceptre of rule, hacker of nations,
ceaseless in fury, ruling by rage,
relentless in pursuit.

The earth, still, mute,
explodes in joy,
even Lebanon's cedars and firs:
'Since you dropped,
the woodchopper will not lop us!'

Sheol below is excited at your coming,
ghosts are woken, chieftains, kings, all
lifted from their thrones ...

43

All will echo:
You too are hollow as us, as us?
Your majesty is come to Sheol
        accompanied by harps.
Your mattress – maggots,
your sheets – worms.

How are you fallen from the sky, morning-star,
smashed to earth, nation-crusher!

Yet you said to yourself:
The sky I'll climb,
beyond the stars set my throne, far north
on the range of eternity
above the highest cloud,
like God . . .

But to Sheol you'll go,
down to the end of the pit.
Those who knew you will look and look again:
Is this a man who shook the earth,
who made kingdoms shake?
who made the earth a wasteland
and its cities ruins?
who let no captive free?

Kings of all nations sleep in honour,
each in his tomb:
But you were hurled from the grave
        like some hideous growth
in sword-torn bloody clothes,
a trampled carcass on the pit's floor.

You will not be buried with the other kings,
for you ruined your land,
killed your people –
no evil children will be named for you . . .

Prepare to slaughter his children
for their fathers' sins!
They must not rise to inherit the earth,
and fill the world with cities . . .

(*Isaiah* 21:4–9; 14:4–21)

The Babylonian revolts, however, encouraged revolts elsewhere. In Judah the hatred of Assyria was expressed through religious change. Hezekiah, Ahaz's son, asserted Judah's religious independence by destroying pagan places of worship and their sacred objects. The revolutionary chain reaction set off by the death of Sargon II in 705 appears once more to have been started by Merodach Baladan, who again led the Babylonians to independence, but this lasted less than a year before the Assyrians regained control. Meanwhile, as the eastern Mediterranean coastal area – Phoenicia, Judah and Egypt – seized the chance to rebel, Hezekiah successfully waged war against the Philistines, who this time had refused to join the anti-Assyrian coalition. As usual, Judah was divided: its revolt was heavily dependent on Egyptian support, particularly for horses and chariots. At this point, Isaiah, by now an old man, reappeared. In a poem attributed to him, he advised Hezekiah to stay clear of the rebellion, and avoid Israel's fate after a similar alliance with Egypt two decades earlier.

THE WARNING

Hoi!
Who go to Egypt for help!
Who trust in horses, chariots and riders
(for these are numerous, powerful)
but not in Kedosh Yisrael –
Yahweh they do not seek.

But he, too, is wise.
He is the cause of this evil.
He does not go back on his word.
He fights the house of the wicked!
He will not stand for their being helped!

For Egypt is man, not God!
their horses flesh, not spirit.
Yahweh will extend his hand –
the helper will stumble, the helped will fall,
and they'll all go down together.

The Lord said this to me.

As the lion growling over its prey
is fearless of a gabble of yelling shepherds,
so God will come down –

to fight on Mount Zion!

Like birds hovering over their young,
Yahweh Zabaot will shield Jerusalem,
and rescue it as he sweeps by!

Children of Israel! Turn back to him,
for you have rebelled
grievously!

For the day will come
when you'll despise your silver gods
and your gods of gold,
shaped for sin with your own hands –
for Asshur will fall by no man's sword
and run from the sword of no-man.
His young men will be slaves.
His rock-like king will vanish in terror.
His princes will shiver
at the sight of Yahweh's banner!

The word of Yahweh
whose fire burns in Zion,
        his furnace in Jerusalem ...

(Isaiah 31)

Isaiah's advice proved to be well-founded, and his hint at the fate of the Assyrians turned out to be true. The Assyrians under Sennacherib, having crushed the revolt of Merodach Baladan, moved south along the coastal plain, defeating Phoenicia and driving swiftly into Philistia, where at Ekron they annihilated a large Egyptian army, the backbone of the revolt. Then, around 701, they turned inland, climbing into the Judean hills, conquering dozens of Hezekiah's fortified towns, including Lachish, taking tens of thousands of captives and, finally, reaching the walls of Jerusalem. According to an inscription of Sennacherib's, Hezekiah was made a prisoner in his own palace, trapped 'like a bird in a cage' (Pritchard, p. 288). Isaiah (1:5–8) might be describing the ruin of Judah in these lines:

The whole head is sick,
the whole heart sorrows –
head to foot,
wounds, bruises, open sores,
unpressed, unbandaged, untreated with oil ...

Your country lies waste.
Your cities are burned down.
You watch your land devoured by strangers,
desolate as after a flood.

And the daughter of Zion remains
like a hut in a vineyard or cucumber-patch –
like a city besieged ...

On the Taylor Prism (Thomas, pp. 66–7), Sennacherib lists the tribute which Hezekiah gave him: gold, silver, precious stones and ivory, among other things, not to speak of his daughters and concubines! The Bible (*II Kings* 18) mentions the gold and silver but not the rest and goes on to describe the Assyrian envoy's call for surrender. His argument is the essence of *chutzpah* as well as shrewd psychological warfare: Assyria was doing the will of Yahweh, this being Isaiah's own claim! However, he then goes on to argue that Yahweh was powerless to defend the Judeans and that Jerusalem would fall.

Though Isaiah had previously counselled against rebellion, he now advised Hezekiah not to give in. This is a rare instance in prophetic poetry in which a prophet, faced with military crisis, does not call for submission and appeasement of a superior foe. This scene, repeated almost verbatim three times, in *Isaiah*, *Kings* and *Chronicles*, is a watershed in Judean history and in the evolution of the prophetic role and image. The prophets, especially in the recent past, had been exceptionally critical of their own society. Now Isaiah suddenly emerged as a great religious-political leader in crisis, an adviser to the king as well as a spokesman for God. Here is his reply to Sennacherib's call for surrender.

ISAIAH'S POEM TO SENNACHERIB

She scorns you, mocks you
behind your back –
the virgin daughter of Jerusalem!

Whom did you curse so loud,
turning your eyes up to heaven
at Kedosh Yisrael?

Adonai you cursed.
Through your servants you bragged:
I've climbed mountains with my chariots!
Into the Lebanon I cut my way,

toppling tall cedars, spruce cypresses.
To the highest point I climbed,
to a thick forest.
I dug and I drank water,
and with a touch of my sole
I dried the moats of siege ...

Haven't you heard?
I decided all this long ago.
Now I've made it happen:
You turn fortified cities to ruins,
and their people, powerless to stop you,
are afraid and ashamed –
blown like plants in the open fields,
or grass on a roof, blighted ...

And I know your comings and goings
and your fury at me –
your fury and arrogance have reached me –

I will stick my hook through your nose
and my bridle in your mouth
and take you back the way you came ...

(Isaiah 37:22–9)

The fate of the Assyrians at Jerusalem in 701 is tantalizingly vague
and, as usual in biblical criticism, the absence of certainty has invited
mountainous speculation, a few verses becoming the subject of entire
books. Some scholars think that two or more episodes may be telescoped
into one. Isaiah's poem to Sennacherib is also quoted in *II Kings*, which
is followed by a prose report: 'that night the angel of God went out
and killed 185,000 in the Assyrian camp' (19:35). It may be that
Hezekiah saved Jerusalem when he paid tribute to Sennacherib, or
that Merodach Baladan or someone else diverted the Assyrians by
stirring up further rebellion in Mesopotamia, or that the Assyrian
army was decimated by plague or a combination of these. Whatever
happened, the Assyrians pulled back without capturing Jerusalem. If
there was a plague, it had the effect described in Psalm 91:

Do not fear
terror by night or the arrow that flies by day,
the plague that stalks in the mist,
or ruin at high noon.

Figure 9   Prisoners of war with Assyrian taskmaster, *c.* 700

A thousand may fall round you,
you won't be touched.

Sennacherib was not led from Jerusalem by the nose, like a captive, but the deliverance of Jerusalem was seen by the Judeans as a sign of the power and mercy of God, of his will to let Judah survive. For this reason, the episode, though minor in the history of the age, is the only one pertaining to a prophet repeated three times in the Bible. This was Judah's only 'victory' over Assyria. Isaiah's role during the siege increased the prestige of the prophets and helped ensure that their message would be preserved. Indeed, Judah's resistance to Assyria was a watershed in the history of prophecy much as Florence's successful resistance to the invading Duke of Milan, Gian Galeazzo Visconti, in 1402 – his forces were struck down by a plague – was crucial in the growth of the Renaissance. Both cases of failed imperialism had a decisive effect on human self-perception: the first was taken as a mark of God's hand in history; the second led to a sharper vision of man's centrality in society, of political liberty and civic virtue.

The position of Judah's victory in the book of Isaiah is also important: it is followed by poems of consolation and the return of Second Isaiah, as if to suggest that Isaiah's prophecy of 701 came true in 539, when Cyrus conquered Babylon. Hosea's simile of Israel as God's wayward but beloved wife also had unceasing relevance to Judah. His poem on the conciliation of husband and wife, though dating from a period prior to the exile, might have given hope that the exiles in Mesopotamia would return to their homes. The renewed marriage contract of God and his people would include the abolition of war and of cruelty to animals, a covenant diametrically opposed to the bellicose Assyrians for whose kings war and hunting were a way of life.

THE RESTORATION

I will seduce her,
lure her to the desert,
speak to her gently.

I will promise her vineyards back
and the valley of Achor – gate of hope ...
She will answer as in her youth,
when she came out of Egypt.

And on that day
I will make a covenant with the wild beasts,
the birds and reptiles –
I will abolish war, break the sword,
and let them sleep in peace.

I will betroth you to me forever.
I will betroth you to me in righteousness,
in justice, mercy and love.
And I will betroth you to me in faith –
And you will know God.

(*Hosea* 2:16–22)

Judah, having come to the edge of annihilation, was now increasingly susceptible to universal principles, as well as to visions of the end of days, which overshadowed petty nationalism. The idea of a 'Day of the Lord' when Yahweh would judge the nations and of a golden age when mankind would live in peace apparently begins in the time of Isaiah. The prophets, tormented by visions of guilt and retribution, largely shifted the criterion of power from a military to a moral sphere in which Yahweh was triumphant. By creating an empire of faith which could survive while territorial empires fell, they 'defeated' the Assyrians and, later, the Babylonians, Greeks and Romans. Whether one believes that they discovered an absolute truth or created a fiction that was believed in and, therefore, became truth, there is no doubt that the prophets were largely responsible for a viable system of faith through which Judeans – and all other peoples, no matter how weak or marginal – could feel themselves to be masters of their destiny. All calamities suffered by Israel and Judah are attributed not to the superior might of other nations, but to their own sins. This meant that the surviving Judeans, far from being at the mercy of random, chaotic forces over which they had little control, had immense power over their fate. The failure of the Judeans to use this power, and their consequent guilt, had forced Yahweh to punish them – so prophetic reasoning went – but they still had the power to repent. By accepting guilt, even if exaggerated, they could open the way to forgiveness and the hope of redemption. The burden of guilt was heavy and long-lasting, but only by stressing the need to accept guilt could the prophets hope to preserve their nation and faith.

It is a striking fact that prophecies of the return of the Israelite exiles are ascribed to each of the four surviving literary prophets of the late eighth century. They signify a powerful bond with Israel, which seems to have been transformed into an idealized phantom nation with which the Judeans identified in anger and guilt and the yearning for its restoration:

> And I will restore the loss of my people, Israel.
> They will rebuild abandoned cities, live in them ...
> never again be uprooted ...
>
> (*Amos* 9:14–15)

> 'Let my sons come trembling
>   from the river lands
> Trembling like a bird from Egypt
>   and a dove from Asshur –
> I will return them to their homes!'
>
> (*Hosea* 11:11)

> ... there will be a highway for the remnant
> of his people in Asshur, as there was for Israel
> when he came out of Egypt.
>
> (*Isaiah* 11:16)

I will surely gather Jacob, all of you.

I will surely gather the remnant of Israel.

(*Micah* 2:12)

These prophecies were not fulfilled, but they created a tradition of hope for Israel's restoration which was so firmly rooted by the time of the fall of Judah that this tradition could be drawn on when the Judeans, too, were exiled, to inspire them to return to their land. The prophets were not always factually correct, but the fall of Israel forced on them an awareness of the need for hope and the *realpolitik* of the spirit. The exile of Israel, and other disasters which followed, served as a lesson to the faithful among the Judeans, subjugated though they were to the Assyrians. It helped strengthen their moral fibre and provided focal points for religious observance. It also enhanced national unity, as well as self-questioning and faith in Yahweh. In this way, Isaiah and his fellow prophets laid the foundation for the survival of the Jews as a distinct people, though uprooted from their homeland.

2

BABYLONIA AND THE FALL OF JUDAH

Isaiah's poetry at the time of the siege of Jerusalem in 701 is the last datable poetry in Hebrew prior to the reign of Josiah (*c.* 640–609). Poems and fragments from the intervening time – prophecies on Babylon or Egypt, for example – might have found their way into the extant prophetic books, but this cannot be proven. In fact, not even the names of prophets have survived from this period. Why this silence? Two major facts about this period suggest an answer: Judah was an Assyrian vassal and her king for over half a century (*c.* 697–642) was Manasseh, Hezekiah's son. Contemporary Assyrian records describe Manasseh as one of twenty-two vassal kings west and south-west of the Euphrates, forced to transport heavy lumber and stone to Nineveh, to offer weighty gifts to the king and to kiss his feet as a sign of subservience (Pritchard, pp. 291, 294). Manasseh undid his father's reforms, possibly under Assyrian pressure. Prophets of Yahweh might have been murdered by Manasseh, for by following Isaiah's message on the ramparts of Jerusalem, they opposed the policy of submission and the adoption of pagan gods and customs. We are told in *II Kings* that Manasseh 'shed very much innocent blood, till he filled Jerusalem from one end to the next' (21:16). Some of this blood might have been that of the prophets: tradition has it that Isaiah was one of Manasseh's victims. (It is also possible that prophets at this time were so slavishly pro-Assyrian that their message was deemed inappropriate to later generations and forgotten.) Manasseh ensured that during his reign Judah would not follow Israel into exile. Yet he is the most vilified king in the Bible for, like his grandfather Ahaz, he sacrificed Judah's religious freedom, and the prophetic tradition resurfaced only after his death.

In Manasseh's time, Assyria reached the height of its power – the mastery over the entire Fertile Crescent with its conquest of Egypt in 663. This unprecedented triumph was followed by an equally astonishing decline. After the death in 627 of Assyria's last great king, Ashurbanipal, Egypt almost immediately regained sovereignty, the Babylonians and Medes rebelled and the Judeans under Josiah reasserted their religious independence and waited for Assyria's death-throes.

The Bible describes Josiah undertaking a massive reform, as Hezekiah had done nearly a century earlier in parallel circumstances. The discovery of the forgotten 'Book of the Law' marks the start of this reform. Josiah destroyed the sacred idols and objects of pagan worship; he abolished sacred prostitution and child-sacrifice; he outlawed mediums and witches; he did away with the provincial sanctuaries (the so-called 'high places'), killed or demoted their priests and centralized Yahweh worship in Jerusalem; and he reinstated the festival of Passover which, according to *II Kings* 23, had not been celebrated, or not properly, for hundreds of years. Apart from these reforms, he restored and encouraged the prophetic tradition, which now entered its second great period. The apocalyptic atmosphere of this age of military upheaval and religious reform is captured by the prophet Zephaniah.

THE AGE OF JOSIAH'S REFORMS

I will sweep the lot off the face of the earth,
sweep man and beast, sweep bird and fish,
idols and their devotees, from the face of the earth!

I will stretch my hand against Judah
and all the people of Jerusalem.
I will put an end to Ba'al and the priests of Ba'al,
the false priests of Yahweh, who worship on roofs –
an army of gods! – those who swear by Yahweh,
by Milcom too, those who turn from Yahweh,
and those who never sought him out.

The day of Adonai Yahweh comes near!
Watch out, he has planned a slaughter!
He has invited his guests!

On the day of Yahweh's slaughter
I will punish the nobles and the king's sons,
who ape foreign dress, the ones who cling

to superstition (leaping over the threshold!),
who fill their master's house with violence and fraud.

On that day, Yahweh declares,
a cry will come from the Fish Gate,
a scream from the suburb, a loud crash from the hills –
Wail, dwellers of Makhtesh! for the traders are ruined,
the money-handlers finished!

On that day I will search Jerusalem with lamps,
punishing those ... sunk in their dregs,
who say: God will do neither good nor bad!
Their wealth will be plundered, their houses laid waste.
If they build houses, they will not live in them.
If they plant vines, they will not drink their wine.

The day of Yahweh comes closer, faster!
Listen! the day of Yahweh:
the bitter screams of warriors!
On that day – a day of fury, of anguish and ruin,
of trumpet blast and battle cries
across the fortified cities and their tall towers –

I will make them suffer. They will walk like the blind,
for they sinned against Yahweh.
Their blood will be cheap as dust, their flesh like dung.
Silver and gold will not save them
on the day of Yahweh's wrath.

All the earth will be devoured with his wrath.
He will make a fearful end of earthlings.

(Zephaniah 1:2–18)

By 614, Nineveh, the Assyrian capital on the Tigris, was besieged. The end came two years later with a combined assault from the Babylonians, Medes and Scythians. The fall of Nineveh was a watershed in ancient history. It is depicted spectacularly by the prophet Nahum. This poetry, with its eyewitness immediacy, its rhythmic energy and alliterative excitement, the colour and savagery of its battle scenes, the great heave of sarcasm, relief and exultation at the end, is magnificently equal to the event – the fall of the most powerful and ruthless empire the world had yet known. In its own way, Nahum's poetry echoes the brutality of Assyria and artistically is a verbal equivalent of the great Assyrian wall reliefs in Nineveh.

Nahum's hatred of Assyria, his lust for revenge, his gloating delight
at Nineveh's fall, are undisguised. His poem captures a moment in
Judah's history when, for the first time in decades, national independence seemed within reach and Judah breathed free of Assyria.
The uniqueness of the poem has to do not only with its superb verbal
pyrotechnics but also with the fact that the period of relief and hope
engendered by Assyria's fall was so short-lived.

THE FALL OF NINEVEH

Hoi!
City of blood!
Bloated with lures
to plunder its prey!

Hark! the whip, the rattle of wheels,
straining horses,
      chariots careening,
         horsemen charging,
sword aflame, the glitter of spears:
the hammering ram has come to your gates –

   Up to the ramparts!
   Watch the way!
     Be strong and of good courage!

          *   *   *

Red the attacker's shield,
warriors decked in scarlet.
Torch-like the chariots flash,
javelins tremble poisonously:
Lightning torches streak.
Chariots frenzied roar in the squares,
the clang of steel in the streets.

Generals summoned
stumble in their march
race to the wall –
but the mantelet is moving

56

Figure 10 Assyrian siege-engine in campaign in southern Iraq, *c.* 728

Broken the river-gates,
the palace floods with fear.
The queen stripped, dragged away –
her handmaids moan like doves,
beat at their breasts.
Nineveh of old was like a tranquil pool –
now her people flee in a panicked stream:

Stop! Stop!
Spoil the silver!
Spoil the gold!

There's no end to the treasure,
no end of the precious wares ...

*   *   *

57

Blasted, blank and bare:
No end of the slain.
Everywhere corpses strewn.
Mountainous dead.
Soldiers stumble on the bodies.

How your shepherds slumber,
king of Asshur!
Your warriors lie in peace.
Your people are scattered over the mountains –
no one gathers them.

There's no balm to ease your pain,
the wound too deep:
All who hear of it
clap their hands in glee ...
for over whom did your evil
scourge not pass?

(from *Nahum* 2, 3)

The fall of Assyria, like its rise a century earlier, completely upset the balance of power in the Fertile Crescent. The Egyptians, in a remarkable turnabout, tried to save their former arch-enemy, Assyria, and went to war against Babylonia in 609. Their apparent motives were to stop the rise of an overly-strong and possibly hostile Babylonia, to preserve Assyria as a valuable buffer against marauding northern tribes, and to keep the cauldron boiling in Mesopotamia. Judah sided with Babylonia, to preserve its independence from Assyria and to gain favour with the emerging superpower. The Egyptian army, under Pharaoh Neco, moved north along the Mediterranean coast and through the plain of Jezreel. The Judean army led by Josiah met him at the pass of Megiddo (the scene of Deborah's victory over the Canaanites some five centuries earlier). The Judeans were defeated, Josiah was killed, and Judah now found itself a vassal of Egypt. The Egyptians deported Jehoahaz, the new king of Judah, and set up his brother, Jehoiakim, as their puppet ruler of Judah. Jehoiakim established a vicious, despotic regime, and persecuted the prophets of Yahweh.

This sudden twist of events was devastating to the faithful Judeans. Josiah had, after all, abolished pagan worship and restored the worship of Yahweh. He is the most approved-of Judean king in the Bible. His cruel end seemed undeserved. At this time, it seems, a literary tradition began in which Yahweh's justice is called into question. The prophets

Habakkuk and Jeremiah were among the first to employ this theme, which reaches its quintessential expression in the book of Job.

SONGS OF GOD'S INJUSTICE

1

If I quarrelled with you,
you'd win, Lord,
though I argued justly:

Why do the wicked make good,
and turncoats live in peace?

You plant them, they take root,
go on to give fruit –
they pay you in lip service
but couldn't care less ...

You know me, Lord,
you've seen and tested me:
Round them up like sheep!
Massacre them!

How long will this land mourn,
and grass die everywhere,
birds and beasts die
for the evil of these men who say:
God has no power over us!

2

How long, Yahweh, do I lament
to your deaf ears?
How long cry *Murder!*
and you not save me?
Why do you show me wrongs,
strife, violence and ruin?
Why do you spread trouble before me?

This is why law shrivels up,
justice loses its eternal force,
why the wicked checkmate the good.

This is why justice is twisted.
                    (*Jeremiah* 12:1–4; *Habakkuk* 1:2–4)

The Judeans, shocked by their defeat and Josiah's death, and by their vassaldom, must have felt that God is not just. As Job puts it (9:22): 'he kills off the good and the wicked alike.' The Egyptian army marched north into Mesopotamia. Their crucial battle with the Babylonians took place in 605 at Carchemish, along the north bank of the Euphrates. The Egyptians were routed by the Babylonian crown prince, Nebuchadrezzar. Ignominiously they were chased south, past Judah, to the Egyptian border. This battle firmly established Babylonian supremacy over the Fertile Crescent and its eclipse of Assyria, which vanished from history. Jeremiah's poem on the battle of Carchemish expresses the Judeans' shortlived delight at the downfall of their enemy and at being released from vassaldom. The Egyptian defeat seemed to confirm once more God's hand in history.

THE BATTLE OF CARCHEMISH

Shield and buckler! Ready!
Polish spears!
Coats of mail!
Infantry! Helmets!
Horses harnessed! Mount!

Advance to battle!

Why do I see them tremble
in retreat,
warriors cut down,
they don't look back when they run,
the terrors round them –
        Yahweh declares!
The swift will not escape,
nor the mighty,
but they stumble, fall
up north, by the Euphrates.

Who swelled up like the Nile
like tossing rivers?
Egypt!
'I will rise, flood the land, destroy
city and dwellers!'

Horses! Leap as you please!
Tumble, chariots, madly about!

Let Egypt's mercenaries come, too,
from Cush and Punt, with shields,
from Lud, with bows!

This is a day
of revenge for Adonai Yahweh Zebaot;
The sword will chew up his foes,
get drunk on their blood!
This −
Yahweh's slaughter, up north
by the Euphrates.

   Crawl up to Gilead,
virgin daughter of Egypt!
to find medicine;
as much as you use, it won't help −
All the nations hear your cry
and your shame
for your men of war have fallen, crashed
against each other.

(Jeremiah 46:3−12)

Figure 11   Scene of slaughter in Assyrian–Elamic wars, c. 663

Egypt's defeat, however, led not to Judean independence, but to the transfer of Judah's vassaldom to Babylonia. This infuriated the Judeans, especially as Josiah's attempt to defend the Babylonians against the Egyptians had originally brought about Judah's vassaldom to Egypt. From the Babylonian viewpoint, the restoration of independence to Judah might have led to the creation of a pro-Egyptian satellite, hostile to Babylonia. Apart from this risk, there was also Babylonia's imperial ambition to conquer the Fertile Crescent as Assyria did. As a result, a powerful pro-Egyptian, anti-Babylonian faction emerged in Judah. Once again, caught in the pincers of superpower rivalry, Judah waited to regain independence.

The chance soon came. In 601, the Babylonians under Nebuchadrezzar began a campaign to conquer Egypt. Using Judah as a warpath, they apparently made free use of their vassal, plundering and destroying as they pleased. The following poem in the book of Joel, which some commentators believe to be a metaphor, might describe this invasion or a similar one. The depiction of invasion as a plague of locusts is found also in accounts of the Midianites (*Judges* 6:5) and the Assyrians (*Isaiah* 33:4).

THE INVASION

Wake up, drunks, and weep!
Groan, wine-guzzlers!
for the drink snatched from your lips.
A numberless horde has reached my land:
His teeth are the teeth of a lion,
his jaws – of a mauling beast.
He has made my vine a waste,
my fig-tree foam with blight.
When he strips it bare and tosses it down
its branches are white.

Wail like a virgin in sackcloth
for the love of her youth.
Wine and flour have vanished
from Yahweh's temple
and the priests who serve him mourn.
Blasted the fields,

the earth laments,
for the corn is plundered, the new wine spoiled,
the oil is bad.

Farmers! Dressers of the vine!
Shrivel in shame and wail
for the wheat and for the barley,
the lost harvest.
Withered the vine and fig
and all the trees of the field –
pomegranate, apple and palm,
and joy has withered ...

(Joel 1:5–12)

The Babylonians and Egyptians clashed on Egypt's border. The Egyptians inflicted heavy losses on their attackers and drove them back. The Babylonian retreat was accompanied by further spoilage of Judah. Jehoiakim, incensed, withheld tribute from Nebuchadrezzar, hoping that the Babylonian setback would forestall an invasion. This was indeed the case for the next two years. During this time, however, Nebuchadrezzar organized small-scale attacks on Judah by the Chaldeans, Arameans, Moabites and Ammonites (*II Kings* 24:2). In 598, Nebuchadrezzar attacked. The advance of his army is described by Jeremiah in the following group of poetic fragments. Once again, as in the earlier prophets, God is depicted punishing his people for their sins.

NEBUCHADREZZAR'S ATTACK

Proclaim this in Judah and Jerusalem!
Shout it out, blow the trumpet through the land –
'Gather all – to the fortified cities!'
Raise the banner for flight to Zion.
Do not wait –
for I bring evil from the north,
and ruin.

A hot wind comes from the desert hills,
too strong to winnow or to cleanse –
It is I who speak in judgement.

Look! They come like clouds,
Their chariots raise a storm,
horses fleet as eagles,
this people from the north!
Clutching bow and spear, they roar
like the sea, they have no mercy –
they ride dressed for battle against you –
daughter of Zion!

A powerful nation, ancient nation
whose language you do not know!
Warriors all,
their quiver – an open grave.
They will eat your harvest, your bread,
sheep and cattle, vine and fig-tree.
Your sons and daughters they will eat ...
and put to the sword
the fortified cities in which you trust.

We have heard what they are like.
Our hands are paralysed.
We tremble like a woman giving birth.

'Avoid the fields!
Do not use the roads!
For the sword of the enemy waits,
        terror on every side!'

Daughter of my people!
Put sackcloth on, roll in ashes,
mourn as for an only son,
bitter lamentation.

'Race through the streets of Jerusalem,
back and forth –
see if you can find a just man,
a man who seeks truth –
and I will pardon her.'

I saw the earth – a void,
and the heavens went dark.
I saw the mountains quake
and the hills tremble.
I saw no man, not even a bird.

I saw forest turned to desert
and all its cities to ruin
for fear of Yahweh ...

Riders!
Archers!

The city empties.
All race for the caves,
    crouch in thickets,
        scramble up cliffs.
The city is left, deserted.

  Plundered one!
Why do you dress in scarlet
and put on ornaments of gold?
Why do you stretch your eyes with paint?
You do it for nothing.
Your lovers despise you.
They are out to kill you.

I hear a cry like the cry of a woman
giving birth for the first time –
the cry of the daughter of Zion,
gasping, her arms flailing –
Oiah li!
I faint before the murderers!

(from Jeremiah 4, 5, 6)

At this time, Jehoiakim died and his 18-year-old son, Jehoiachin, was king when Nebuchadrezzar defeated Judah and captured Jerusalem in 597. Imitating Assyrian policy, Nebuchadrezzar deported many Judeans – the king, the soldiery, craftsmen, aristocracy and other leading figures – to Babylonia. The common people, thought to have little importance, were allowed to stay. Zedekiah, Judah's last king, was set up by the Babylonians in place of Jehoiachin. Jeremiah viewed the young king's fate with horror and disgust.

THE FATE OF JEHOIACHIN

This shattered idol, spurned –
This ... Coniah!
Why were he and his family

65

taken, cast off to an unknown land!

Land!

    Land!

        Land!

Listen! The word of Yahweh:

'Write this man off as barren.
Nothing will come of him, ever,
   nor from his offspring –
   a king to sit on David's throne,
to rule Judah!'

                (*Jeremiah* 22:28–30)

The other great prophet in the age of Jeremiah was Ezekiel. Like Jeremiah, Ezekiel was a priest as well as a prophet. Unlike Jeremiah, he was included among the exiles driven to Babylonia with Jehoiachin in 597. His prophecies are the only ones in the Bible known to have taken place outside the land of Israel. His prophetic career began shortly before the destruction of the Temple in Jerusalem and continued for at least twenty years. Like Jeremiah, he preached a message of political appeasement – this, perhaps, was inevitable in view of the precarious status of the exiles – but, also like Jeremiah, he stressed the need to preserve religious integrity and moral strength.

As an exile in Babylonia, Ezekiel was vehemently opposed to Judean resistance to Babylonian rule, knowing that the result would probably be the total destruction of Judah. The following allegorical poem of Ezekiel's expresses his lack of sympathy with Judean militancy, seeing it as aimless violence leading to entrapment and exile. The imagery which he uses is virtually identical with that found in the statues and wall reliefs which he must have seen in exile.

DIRGE FOR THE LIONS OF JUDAH

What is your mother?
A lioness.
Crouching among lions, raising her young.
One of her cubs grew into a lion.
He learned to catch prey.
He ate men.
Nations banded against him.
They trapped him in their pit.

They dragged him in hooks
to Egypt.

His mother lost hope of his return.
She took one of her young.
She made him into a lion.
He wandered among the lions.
He learned to catch prey.
He ate men.
He ravaged their widows.
He ruined their cities.
He desolated the whole land
with the force of his roaring.

Nations banded against him
from every side.
They spread their net across him.
He was trapped in their pit.
They put him in a cage with hooks.
They brought him to the king of Babylon,
that his roar be heard no longer
over the mountains of Israel.

(Ezekiel 19:2–9)

Figure 12   Lion about to be killed, *c.* 645

In common with Jeremiah, Ezekiel was fearful of military alliances, especially with Egypt, which endangered Judah's survival. Egypt, having suffered a crushing defeat at Carchemish in 605, was eager to fight Babylonia again, and cautiously willing to support Judah in revolt. At this time a nationalist movement, guided by the new nobility and their prophets, grew in Judah, pinning its hopes mainly on a Judean–Egyptian alliance. The nationalists hoped to return Jehoiachin and the exiles, and to restore the sacred objects taken by Nebuchadrezzar from the Temple in Jerusalem. History had shown that alliances with Egypt did not work – they had led to the fall of Israel in 720, and to the near-destruction of Judah two decades later. Now history was repeating itself and Judah, it seemed, had learned nothing. The following poem forms part of an elaborate series of prophecies of Ezekiel's against Egypt. As in the time of the Assyrian conquests in the late eighth century, Egypt could not save Judah and was itself conquered; yet Ezekiel has far less sympathy for Egypt than Isaiah had over a century earlier. It is likely that the newly reinstated Passover festival offered an outlet against Egypt at this time and later, for it recalls the plagues against Egypt, such as the river turning to blood and pitch darkness, which appear in Ezekiel's poem.

DOOM-SONG FOR EGYPT

I am against you,
Pharaoh king of Egypt –
big crocodile crouching in the Nile:
'This is my river. I made it!'

You put on lion's airs,
water-bound monster,
pouncing in your rivers
fouling the water,
making a stink ...

I'll put your jaws in hooks
and haul you out,
fish clinging to your scales,
hurl you into the desert,
you and your small-fry too –

you'll have no decent burial,
food for birds and beasts ...

All Egypt will know:
I am the Lord.

To the mountains your flesh!
To the valleys your excellent coat!
Mountain streams will water the earth
with your blood –

Sun and stars I'll cover in cloud,
the moon will give no light.
I will make your land pitch black,
says the Lord God.

Son of man!
Wail for the masses of Egypt!
Cast him down with nations doomed
to the lower depths
of Sheol!

Are you, Egypt, prettier than they?
Go down, lie with the godless
who fell by the sword!

(from *Ezekiel* 29, 32)

Meanwhile, as the Judean kingdom reached its end, Jeremiah came to his full strength as a poet of unique sensitivity and courage. On the basis of a handful of lyrics, flung almost inadvertently into a chaotic sea of prophecy, he emerges as one of the greatest of confessional poets. His fragmented poems are the outpourings of a man entrusted with a message of doom: the total destruction of Judah by the Babylonians and the ruin of the Temple in Jerusalem. Jeremiah was hated by many of his own people for being a prophet of disaster: his writings were burned, he was imprisoned, tortured and threatened with death. Yet, seduced and overpowered by the word of God, he could not evade his mission.

What did he feel in such hideous circumstances? Jeremiah gives unrivalled insight into his complex psychology, the ambivalent sense of exhilarating privilege and devastating futility; pain, self-pity, and a Job-like wish for death; disgust at his people, lust for revenge, bitterness towards God. No other biblical personality displays personal feeling so intimately and vividly. As a confessional poet, Jeremiah is the most human of biblical characters.

Jeremiah's public and private life was one long tragedy. Though patriotic and God-fearing, he knew that Judah was powerless against Babylonia. He preached submission and the acceptance of exile, a message with far-reaching consequences for the Jews. He saw that the future lay with the exiles in Babylonia. In a letter to them he wrote: 'seek the peace of the city where I have exiled you, pray for it to God, for in its peace will you have peace' (29:7). He even described the Babylonian king, Nebuchadrezzar, the author of Judah's destruction, as the 'servant' of the Lord, fulfilling His word – in much the same way Isaiah had described the Assyrians as God's punitive agents in destroying Israel over a century beforehand. So provocative and unpopular were his views that during the siege of Jerusalem, Jeremiah was kept under guard; only with the fall of Jerusalem was he freed, by personal order of Nebuchadrezzar.

As in the case of Hosea and Ezekiel, Jeremiah used his unhappy personal life to symbolize the state of the nation. He obeyed a divine commandment not to marry – there was no point in having a family which was doomed. Still, like all the great prophets, Jeremiah also offered a message of hope. He predicted the return of the exiles to their land. He even bought a plot of land in his home town of Anathoth, near Jerusalem, as a sign of his God-given confidence that this would happen. His prediction that one day 'the sound of rejoicing, of bride and groom, will be heard in the towns of Judah and the streets of Jerusalem' (33:10–11) is enshrined in the Jewish wedding ceremony. There is great pathos in this prophecy, as in many others of Jeremiah: to his mind, his tragic life could be compensated and justified only by the survival of the Jews.

Jeremiah's most moving and original oracles are not his attacks on Judah and other nations (in which he is clearly influenced by earlier prophets, such as Hosea, Micah and Isaiah), but those written (or spoken) in moments of self-doubt and despair. It may be that only by descending into the dark turmoil within himself could he summon up the strength to offer hope to a people in a seemingly hopeless state.

CONFESSIONS OF JEREMIAH

1

You lured me, O Lord
and I was lured.
With your strength you got
what you wanted:

Morning to night I am mocked,
a laughing-stock to the world.
For I cannot help but cry:
    Murder! Theft!
The Lord's word has brought me nothing
    but insult and shame.

I said: 'I'll forget him,
no longer speak in his name.'
But he stayed in my heart
    like a fire
shut in my bones.
I am tired of holding it back.
I cannot.

Many I've heard slander me –
terror all round.
Even those I know well
wait for me to slip:

'Let us denounce him,
We'll try and lure him
    to his fall
We'll have our revenge.'

But the Lord is with me still
like a ruthless man of war.
Those who come at me
will stumble and fail,
their shame will be forever.

O Lord of Hosts
who tests the good,
who sees the heart within –
show me your vengeance
for I have brought you
my quarrel.

2

Cursed be the day of my birth.
Cursed the man

71

who gladdened my father, saying:
'You have a son!'
May he be like the cities
destroyed by the Lord, mercilessly.
May he hear a cry in the morning –
              a shriek at noon –
for not killing me in the womb,
making my mother my grave,
the birthplace of my eternity.
Why was I born to see such grief
and sorrow, to live my days in shame?

3

Sorrow sweeps over me
              my heart is sick.
My people cry out in a distant land.
'Is Yahweh not in Zion,
is her King not there?'
   (*Why did they enrage me with their idols . . .
        their foreign nothings?*')

The harvest is over,
      summer has gone,
            and we have not been saved.

I am broken by my people's ruin.
I am filled with dark dismay.

In Gilead is there no medicine,
no doctor? Why are my people not
healed?

If my head were a store of water
and my eyes a fountain of tears,
I would cry day and night for the slain
of my people.

If only I had an inn
      in the desert
I would abandon my people,
            treacherous adulterers . . .

4

You know, Lord!
Remember me, come to me, avenge me!
Don't do away with me!
    In your mercy,
know – I have suffered disgrace
        for your sake.
When your word came, I swallowed it
it brought me joy,
for I was called in your name, Lord
        God of Hosts
I had no other joy.
Because of you I sat alone, because
you filled me with rage.
Why does my pain go on and on,
my wound incurable?

Will you be
like a brook that goes dry on me?

5

Heal me, save me, Lord,
for I praise you.

They say: 'Where is the word of God?
Let it come!'
But I have not given up so quickly.
I do not want disaster.
You know:
I spoke your word honestly.
Do not be my ruin.
You are my shelter in trouble.

Put my enemies to shame, not me.
Terrify them, not me.
Bring them bad days.
Crush them twice over.
(From *Jeremiah* 8, 15, 17, 20)

Ezekiel had little of Jeremiah's lyric genius. Poetically the weakest of
the major prophets – most of his book consists, in fact, of prose or
prose-poetry – Ezekiel, nevertheless, had a gift for allegory, doggedly
driving home a message, using a single image at a time. He was not a
great innovator. Many of the elements in his work appear in the

writings of the earlier prophets. Yet he built on their ideas and extended them, occasionally with striking results. The theophany of the opening chapters, for example, has precedents in earlier writings, such as those of Isaiah, but in its awesome grandeur and detail (influenced, perhaps, by the great monuments of Mesopotamian art) it is unique. Similarly, his depiction of the harlotry of Israel and Judah derives partly from Hosea, but he transforms this poetic idea into a stunning allegory of corruption. His oracles on Tyre and Egypt are worthy of comparison with the finest of Isaiah's prophecies to the nations. In his message of hope, too, Ezekiel may be compared with previous prophets. Yet his account of the resurrection of the dry bones, symbolizing the return of the Israelites to their land, is the most remarkable of the prophecies of hope.

Finally, in acting out, in symbolic form, catastrophic events of the future, Ezekiel is not unlike other prophets. Isaiah (20:2–4), for example, was divinely commanded to go naked for three years to symbolize the fate of Egypt and Ethiopia at the hands of the Assyrians: they would be sent naked to exile. Jeremiah (27:2–8) was told, similarly, to wear a yoke to symbolize the future servitude of Judah and other nations to Babylonia. Still, in comparison with these, Ezekiel's symbolic acts are more systematic, stranger and more tragic. He is told, for instance, to go through the motions of putting Jerusalem to siege, as if in a game; to put himself on a strict diet for 390 days, to symbolize the siege and famine; to 'escape' from his home stealthily by night, as a fugitive would; to sigh and moan bitterly for the ruin of the Temple in Jerusalem.

But then he is told that his wife will die – as symbol of the destruction of the Temple – and that he is not to mourn her, presumably as a sign that the national disaster is beyond the bounds of human grief.

Ezekiel occasionally displays an emotional rigidity rare in the Bible, a mechanical quality in his imagery and in set pieces such as the vision of God on his chariot, the details of Temple architecture, and the eschatological vision of the wars of Gog and Magog. In the opening scene, the sky is like the colour of 'the terrible ice' – a coldness which reappears when the prophet is told not to mourn his wife. Even by the norms of the biblical world, Ezekiel seems at least slightly disturbed, though it was not uncommon for prophets to be linked with madmen. However, it is impossible to judge to what extent the sense of emotional attenuation was brought on by defeat and exile and to what extent it originated in other, personal emotional difficulties which acted as a microcosmic counterpart to the larger tragedy. As the only Hebrew prophet exiled to Mesopotamia whose writings have survived, Ezekiel conveys the sense of awkwardness, frustration and derangement felt by many of the exiles, though his fine use of Hebrew is a harbinger of the survival of Hebrew in the diaspora.

EZEKIEL: THE LIVING SYMBOL

1

And you! Son of Man!

Find a brick, engrave it with a city – Jerusalem.
Put it to siege, build a fort, pile up a mound
to attack it, set up camps against it, battering rams
all round. And you – take an iron plate, set it up,
an iron wall, between you and the city, set your face
against it, put it to siege – this will be a sign
for the House of Israel!

2

And you!

Take wheat, barley and beans, lentils, millet and spelt.
Put them in a pot. Make yourself bread for 390 days
(when you are to lie solely on your left side),
an average of nine ounces a day, to be eaten at fixed times.
Drink water by the quart at fixed times.
Prepare your food like barley cakes, baked on human dung,
in public. – In this way the children of Israel
will eat their bread – unclean, among the nations
where I will drive them.

3

Son of Man!

Tremble as you eat bread. Worry as you drink water.
Tell the other exiles: this is what Adonai Yahweh says
to the people of Jerusalem on Israel's soil –
they will eat bread in fear and drink water in despair,
for the land will be stripped by the rage
of its inhabitants.

4

And you! Son of Man!

Get your things ready for exile.

Exile yourself before their eyes, by day –
perhaps they will see – the bitter rebels.
Then, at dusk, go out again, as if to exile.
Make sure they watch as you dig through the wall,
escape in the dark, pack on your shoulder, face hidden.
Don't set eyes on the ground!
For I have made you a sign for the House of Israel.

5

And you! Son of Man!

Find a sword, sharp as a barber's razor,
pass it across your head and beard
take scales to divide the hair:
burn a third in the city after the siege
beat a third with the sword round the city,
scatter a third to the wind –

I will thrust them with my sword!

6
And the word of Yahweh came to me:

Son of Man!
I am going to take the delight
of your eyes, in a plague.
Do not lament or cry, hold back your tears.
Stifle your groans, do not mourn.
Put on your turban, put on your shoes.
Don't cover your face, do not eat the bread
of mourners ...

And I spoke to the people in the morning,
and my wife died at dusk.

The next morning I did as I was told,
and the people asked me:
What do all these things mean to us?
And I replied: The word of the Lord came to me:
Tell the House of Israel I will profane

76

my Temple ... and Ezekiel will be a sign
to you ...

(From *Ezekiel* 4, 5, 12, 24)

Ignoring the warnings of Jeremiah and Ezekiel, the Judean nationalists, with the support of their king, Zedekiah, chose to fight Babylonia. Backed by Egypt and with the help of Phoenicia and Transjordanian nations, the revolt in Judah broke out around 590. Within two years, Jerusalem was under siege, and Egyptian intervention offered only a short reprieve. In 586, Nebuchadrezzar's troops captured Jerusalem, burned the city down, destroyed the Temple and exiled many of the inhabitants to Babylonia. Zedekiah and his family were caught trying to escape. His sons were executed in front of him, then his eyes were gouged out and he was carried in chains to Babylonia. The following poem, from *Lamentations*, traditionally attributed to Jeremiah, describes Judah in defeat.

LAMENT FOR JUDAH

Remember, Lord, what befell us,
see our shame!
Our land and homes in strangers' hands ...

Orphans we became, our mothers – widows.
Silver we paid for water.
Wood we bought – at a price.
Pursued, we had no peace.
   We begged bread
   from Egypt and Asshur!

Our fathers' sins we bore.
Ruled by slaves, we had no saviour.
Our food we got at risk of death
   by the desert sword.
Our skin burned like an oven –
    fever of starvation

Women in Zion raped, virgins,
   in the towns of Judah.
Our princes hung by the hands.
Old men abused.
The young made to slave at the mill,
   to stagger under piles of wood.

The old abandoned the city gate;
the young, their song.
And we – our joy is gone.
Our crown is fallen.

Oi na lanu – we have sinned!

These things have made us sick.
      Our eyes glower:
On the waste of mount Zion
         jackals prowl ...

But you, O Lord, reign forever!
Why do you forever forget us?
Why do you abandon us?
Return us, Yahweh, to you.
Let us be restored,
as we were ...

Or – are you so furious at us?
Do you abhor us so completely?

                              (*Lamentations* 5)

The Babylonians, however, did not wish to destroy Judah totally, but
to control it. They set up a short-lived government under Gedaliah,
whose murder around 582 ended the last vestige of Judean self-rule.
(Jewish tradition to this day retains the annual fast of Gedaliah between
the High Holy Days.) The collapse of Judah led to a third and final
deportation of its inhabitants to Babylonia, and a mass exodus to Egypt
of impoverished refugees and nationalists fearing reprisal. Jeremiah was
forced to accompany them and apparently died in Egypt.

For governmental purposes, Nebuchadrezzar annexed part of Judah's
territory to the province of Samaria. The Edomites, who lived in the desert
south-east of the Dead Sea, absorbed the rest. The Edomite settlement of
Judah was a crowning humiliation. Edom, at various times in the past,
had been a vassal of the Israelites, and had always been looked upon as
an enemy and rival (the story of Jacob and Esau is an allegory of this
relationship). With the invasion of the Edomite squatters, as the Judeans
saw them, Judah reached rock bottom. The following poem by Obadiah
ascribes the eventual fall of Edom to its treachery. It closes with the hope
that the Israelites would return to their land.

Figure 13   Torture of Judean prisoners, Lachish, 701

THE CHARGE AGAINST EDOM

This is what Adonai Yahweh said to Edom.
We heard it from the Lord, through an envoy
sent to the nations, saying:
Let us make war on Edom!

I will cut you down to size,
contemptible nation!
Who live high in the rock-clefts,
lifted up by pride, saying,
Who can bring me down?
If you soared like an eagle to build your nest

79

up among the stars –
I would bring you down!

If thieves stole in
        plunderers by night,
They would take no more than they wanted!
If grape pickers came,
        they'd leave a bit over!
But how Esau is stripped bare,
even his hidden treasures!

Your allies have led you to the brink,
you've been hoodwinked –
trapped by the ones you feed,
stupid as they are ...

Shall I not destroy the wise men of Edom,
and the wisdom of Mount Esau?

Your warriors will tremble in Teman.
They will not stop the slaughter on the mountain.

Shame will engulf you.
For the violence done to your brother Jacob,
you will be exterminated!

The day you stood by
when strangers broke his gates
        and plundered ...

When lots were cast for Jerusalem,
you joined in.

How could you watch, gladly,
and talk big?
How could you swarm through the gates
and take spoil?
How could you stand at the crossroads,
murdering refugees,
turning captives in?

The day of Yahweh comes closer
for all nations
What you did will be done to you.

As you drank to the ruin of my holy mountain,
nations will drink to your ruin ...

A remnant will come back to Mount Zion –
it will be holy.
Jacob will inherit his land.
He will burn,
and Esau will go up like straw
till there's nothing left ...

And the kingdom will be Yahweh's.

(Obadiah 1–18, 21)

After the fall of Jerusalem, Nebuchadrezzar began a thirteen-year siege of Tyre, which in the eighth century had been forced by the Assyrians to submit and pay tribute but was never totally defeated and destroyed. The fall of Tyre inspired some of Ezekiel's finest poetry, more impressive in fact than any surviving work of his on the fall of Jerusalem. Writing in Babylonia, Ezekiel achieves a delicate balance in acknowledging the full military achievement of Babylonia – he even names Nebuchadrezzar – while also attributing the victory to God. (Isaiah, in contrast, excludes the victorious Assyrians from his poem on Tyre, on pp. 34–5 above.) Exile had clearly made the Judeans more cosmopolitan – Ezekiel, for example, has an extraordinarily detailed grasp of Tyre's network of trade – and also more sensitive to Babylonian imperial interests. Still, they did not give up their own unique theological interpretation of history, which enabled them both to submit to the Babylonian aggressor and to retain cautious distance. The relish and detail with which Ezekiel depicts the fall of a former ally, perfidious at times, perhaps, but hardly as hateful as the Babylonians, suggests that his underlying, even unconscious, wish might have been the fall of Babylonia. As in previous poems, notably by Isaiah, there is effective use of a refrain to define units of poetry and to convey the mood of a dirge.

THE FALL OF TYRE

Since Tyre said of Jerusalem:
Aha! The gate of nations is broken
      swung round to me –
I'll fill the space of its ruin!
The Lord God says:
I am against you, Tyre,

81

I will raise nations like tidal waves
to knock your walls and towers down,
even your dust will I scrape off,
leave you a bare rock
where fishermen cast their nets!

I have spoken, says the Lord.
She will be a spoil to nations,
her daughter-towns on the mainland
put to the sword –
and they will know I am the Lord.

I will bring to Tyre Nebuchadrezzar king of Babylon
from up north, king of kings,
horse and chariot,
horsemen and a vast army.
He will put to the sword her daughter-towns,
build siege-wall and earth-ramp
                          against you,
lift great shields,
             axe and battering ram,
break wall and tower!

The dust his horses raise
will bury you.
The clang of his chariot-wheels
will shiver your walls.
When he bursts through the gates,
trampling, killing all before him,
your stout pillars will drop!

They will take your riches,
your cheap wares too.
They'll knock your pretty houses down,
your stone, wood, dust –
    sweep into the sea.

I will silence your song.
Your harps will never play again.
I will make you a bare rock
for fishermen to cast nets,
never to be rebuilt.

I will make you a terror
and you will be no more.

'I am perfection of beauty!'
you, Tyre, said.
The seas' heart your borders,
your builders made perfect your beauty:
Cypress from Senir – your boards,
your mast – cedars of Lebanon.
Oak of Bashan – your oars,
your deck – ivory in Cyprus pine.
Embroidered Egyptian linen – your sail and banner.
Your cabin-tent – blue and purple cloth
          from the isles of Elisha.
The men of Sidon and Arvad – your rowers.
Your captains – the wise old men of Geval ...

All sailors and ships you had working for you,
soldiers from Persia, Lud and Punt,
helmet and shield they hung on your walls –
                this was your beauty!

But your rowers took you to the open sea,
the east wind broke you
in the sea's heart.

Your wares and wealth and trade,
sailors, captains, carpenters, traders, soldiers, all
plunge in the sea's heart.
The day you sink,
the shore will shiver
at the sound of your pilots' shrieks.
Sailors, oarsmen jump ship,
reach land in tears,
roll in ash, pour dust on head,
tear their hair, put on sackcloth,
weep this bitter lament:

Who is silent as sea-bound Tyre?
You gladdened many nations with your trade.
Your vast wealth and wares made kings rich.
Now broken by the sea,
          sunk to the depth –

Figure 14 Assyrian warship, probably built and manned by Phoenicians,
c. 700

your markets and men have gone down with you.
The islands are stunned,
their kings terrified, furious.
Merchants whistle at your fate –

> *You have become a terror*
> *and will be no more.*

Son of Man!

Say this to the prince of Tyre:
Because in your pride you said 'I am God,
I sit on God's throne in the heart of seas' –
but in truth you're a man, not God,
though you thought you had a god's heart –
wiser than Daniel! no secret kept from you! –
and your wisdom got you wealth,
and you got gold and silver
in your wisdom in trade
you increased your wealth
and were proud of it –

84

Therefore, says the Lord,
as you thought you had a god's heart,
I will set strangers against you, tyrants' swords,
set against your splendid wisdom
to profane that splendour!
They'll drag you down to drown
in the heart of the seas.

Will you still declare before you die
'I am God' to your killers?
For in their hands you are man, not God!
Shameful deaths you will die
by the hands of strangers.

I have spoken, says the Lord.

*You have become a terror
and will be no more.*
(from *Ezekiel* 26, 27, 28)

3

PERSIA AND JUDAH'S RESTORATION

In a barrel-vaulted underground building not far from the Ishtar Gate in Babylon, cuneiform documents were excavated nearly a century ago which name King Jehoiachin of Judah as well as other exiles from Judah and many other nations (Pritchard, p. 308). Potentially a focal point of Judean nationalism, Jehoiachin remained a prisoner until the death of Nebuchadrezzar in 562. Among the Judeans, the traditional hope for the return of the exiled Israelites remained alive and found renewed expression. The following prophecies of Jeremiah and Ezekiel date from the early part of the exile. As with the prophets of the eighth century, notably Hosea and Isaiah, they draw on highly emotive themes – the love of parents for their lost children, and the wish to bring the dead back to life – to convey the universal longing of the exile to return to his homeland.

POEMS OF HOPE

1

The word of Yahweh:

Listen!
Bitter sobs and laments in Ramah ...
Rachel weeps for her sons.
She won't be consoled
for they are gone ...

Do not cry: reward will come
for your labour.
They will return from enemy land.
There's hope for you yet.
Your sons will come back to their land.

I have heard Ephraim groan:
You chastened me
like an untrained calf.
Take me back,
for you are my God.
I repented after I turned from you,
I have learned my lesson – I kicked myself
in utter shame, for the disgrace
of my youth.

Is not Ephraim my dear son?
The one I played with – I remember,
no sooner do I start to talk of him.
And my heart goes out to him ...

2

The hand of Yahweh on me;
I was blown to the bone-filled valley.

Round and round he took me ...
So many bones, all so dry.

Son of Man:
Can these bones live? he asked.
My Lord, Yahweh, you know.

He said: Prophesy to these bones.
Say: 'I'll give you flesh, veins, skin.
I'll breathe in you the breath of life,
and you will know I am the Lord.'

So I prophesied.
I heard a sound, a rattling.
The bones joined together,
veins, flesh and skin appeared –
but there was no breath in them.

Then he said: Prophesy to the wind!
Prophesy, Son of Man!
Say: 'Come from the four winds.
Fill these slaughtered men with the breath of life!'

So I prophesied.

Breath filled them.
They stood, a huge crowd.

He said: Son of Man!
These bones are the people of Israel.
Some say our bones are dry,
      our hope is lost,
            we're clean cut off.

Prophesy! Tell them:
I will open your graves and bring you to life.
I will bring you back to the Land of Israel!
                    (*Jeremiah* 31:14–19; *Ezekiel* 37:1–12)

The hope of national revival grew after the death of Nebuchadrezzar, which, like the deaths of the Assyrian kings, triggered off both internal discord and revolutionary fervour in the empire, leading ultimately to the fall of Babylonia in 539. One of the few facts known about the Judean exiles occurred around this time. Evil-Merodach, Nebuchadrezzar's successor, released Jehoiachin from prison in 561 and gave him a position of importance in the Babylonian court. This unexpected act might have arisen partly from the new king's sympathy with Jehoiachin, who was no longer a threat as a figurehead for Jewish nationalism. But it might also have been intended to curry favour with the Judean minority, whose importance was growing with time, and whose support was desirable amid the uncertainties caused by Nebuchadrezzar's death. If this was Evil-Merodach's strategy, it failed as he was assassinated shortly after, as was his successor. Finally, Nabonidus, the last king of Babylonia (552–539), came to the throne amid internal and external discontent. The weakness of the Babylonian empire as well as the token recognition of Jehoiachin helped turn the Judeans' thoughts to their homeland.

The tradition of return might have faded, however, as the Judeans adapted to Babylonia, which in many respects possessed the most attractive and advanced civilization in the world. Allowed to live in peace and relative comfort, they might eventually have assimilated and intermarried and, like Israel, disappeared as a national and religious entity had Babylonia not fallen when it did.

In the mid-sixth century, a local Persian king, Cyrus II, conquered the Median kingdom south of the Caspian Sea; then he moved to Asia Minor and defeated Lydia (*c.* 546). In control of territories north and east of Babylonia, Cyrus closed in on the crumbling empire. In 539, he defeated the Babylonian army at Opis, on the Tigris. A few weeks later, the city of Babylon surrendered without a fight. (According to legend, Cyrus diverted the waters of the Euphrates so that his army could enter Babylon across the dry river-bed.) The fall of Babylon is depicted graphically in the book of Jeremiah. Here, as in the prophetic accounts of the Assyrians and the Babylonians, the Persians are described as God's agents, his 'hammer and sword'. The closing lines allude to the international slave-labour which had built the city of Babylon.

THE FALL OF BABYLON

Yahweh opened his armoury,
gripped weapons of rage – he has work
in the land of Chaldeans!

A sword on the Chaldeans! cries Yahweh,
On Babylon's men, her princes and sages!
A sword on her sorcerers, looking like fools!
A sword on her warriors, terrified!
A sword on horse and chariot!
On her mercenaries, weak as women!
A plundering sword on her treasures!
A sword on her waters, drying them up! ...

Look! An army on horseback
riding from the north!
Clutching bow and spear, cruel as the sea,
set for war against you, daughter of Babylon!

You are my shatterer, Yahweh says,
My hammer and sword – to shatter nations,
to break kingdoms,
to shatter horse and rider, chariot and rider,
men and women, young and old,
sheep and shepherd, ox and farmer,
noble and viceroy ...

Before your very eyes
I will repay Babylon and the Chaldeans
the wrong they did Zion!

Thus the men of Zion: My rage on Babylon!
And Jerusalem: My blood on Chaldea!

Crushed I am, consumed by Babylon,
swallowed by Nebuchadrezzar, the monster ...

Let not the archer bend his bow!
   Let him not rise in his coat of iron!
   Have no pity on his young men!
   Destroy them all!

       *   *   *

The warriors of Babylon
fight no more
houses on fire
   bars broken
      strength gone
they crouch in the citadels,
      weak as women ...

Runner to runner
word comes to the king:

   The city is lost
   on every side,
   bridges taken,
   bulwarks burned,
   soldiers terrified ...

Yahweh Zebaot speaks:

The wide walls of Babylon will be razed
to the earth,
her huge gates burned –
Nations will have worked for nothing,
wearied themselves for the fire ...
                (from *Jeremiah* 50, 51)

Cyrus proceeded to invent a form of enlightened imperialism radically
different from those of Assyria and Babylonia, and more successful –
the Persian empire lasted longer than any empire prior to the Romans.
This imperialism was characterized not just by military power and
good administration, but also by tolerance and fairness. Cyrus treated
his conquered subjects kindly, allowed them a generous measure of
self-rule, maintained the diplomatic fiction that their gods had willingly
given him his victories, retained their languages, respected their insti-
tutions and treasures, restored their religious shrines; and he reversed

Figure 15 Demolition of a city in Assyrian–Elamic wars, *c.* 645

the Assyrian/Babylonian policy of deportation. In 538, he published an edict of liberation allowing the exiles to return to their homes. He thus permitted the Jews to return to their land, ordered the Temple to be rebuilt (with the help of Persian funds) and the Temple treasures plundered by Nebuchadrezzar to be returned. He put Jehoiachin's son, Sheshbazzar, in charge of this operation. These events seemed little short of miraculous, and they set off the third and final great wave of biblical prophecy. Cyrus was regarded by many Judeans as a messiah. The sudden fall of Babylonia and the edict of liberation revived the suppressed grief of the Judeans for their homeland and their anger at the Babylonians and the exile, however comfortable it had been. Psalm

137, with its terrible curse of Babylonia and yearning for Jerusalem, is apparently set against this background:

> If I ever forget you, Jerusalem –
> may my right hand be paralysed!
> May I be struck dumb
> if you are no longer chief of my joys!

Though they did not forget Jerusalem, most of the Babylonian Jews chose to stay in Babylonia under Persian rule. Judah had little to offer but the memory of bygone glory and ignominy such as that of the Edomite occupation. Now the land was waste and full of ruins. Life there was hard and dangerous. Only a relatively small number were inspired to return. Under the leadership of Zerubbabel, a grandson of Jehoiachin, and the high priest Joshua, about 50,000 retraced the five-hundred-odd miles to their homeland. The mood of the age is captured by Second Isaiah, in poetry inspired by Cyrus's victories and the hope of return to Zion.

POEM TO CYRUS

> God's word to Cyrus, anointed as saviour –
> whose right hand I made strong to crush nations,
> break the might of kings,
> open doors, leave no gate barred:
>
> Before you I will go to make straight the road,
> smash bronze gates, split iron bars,
> give you hidden treasure
>   lifted from the dark –
> so you will know: I am God of Israel
> who calls you by name, for Jacob
> my servant, Israel my chosen. I call you by name,
> though you do not know me.
>
> I am God, there is no other. No other.
> I form light. I create the dark.
>   I make peace. I create evil.
> I, God, make all these.
> If the sky rains justice
> and the earth flowers with charity,
>   with fruit of victory,

I, God, make all this.

Hoi!
Who quarrels with his maker?
Who's heard a potsherd
pick a quarrel with its potter?
    'What are you doing?'
    'Your work has no handles!'

Hoi!
Who says to a father:
    'Why do you have children?'
or, to a woman:
    'Why do you go through labour?'

This is what the Lord says,
Holy One of Israel, his Maker:
Ask *me* what the future will bring my sons, my creations!
It was I who made the earth and mankind.
My hand stretched out the heavens,
    ordered their stars,
I lifted Cyrus to victory,
straightened all his roads thereto.
He will build my city.
He will free my exiles,
    and take no payment, no bribe.

This is the word of the Lord of Hosts:
Egypt's wealth,
Cush's wares
and of the tall Sabeans
will be yours –
they'll pass you in chains,
bow to you, pray to you:

'God is in you only.
There is none but he!
Yes, you are a God in hiding,
saviour of Israel!'

In shame they'll pass, stunned,
the idol makers too,

but Israel is saved for all time –
will not be ashamed,
ever!

(Isaiah 45:1–17)

The anonymous prophet saw the return as a recreation of the broken
'marriage' between God and his people. He denounces the worship of
foreign gods and affirms the universal power of Yahweh. The exiles'
wish to return to Zion had eroded. The prophet's message of consolation
was needed to overcome their reluctance to return.

CONSOLATION

1

Take comfort, comfort ... my people ...
your God will say.
Talk gently to Jerusalem.
Tell her the exile is over, her sin forgiven.
For at Yahweh's hand she served double time
for all her sins ...

Listen! A voice!

Clear Yahweh's road in the desert!
Straight through the plain –
Lift every valley, level each hill,
make the winding ways straight
and the rugged land –
Yahweh's glory will be revealed.
All flesh will know he has spoken.

Cry out! the voice declares.
What shall I cry? I ask.

All flesh is grass,
all its beauty like a blossom in a field ...
As grass dies, as the flower withers,
touched by the breath of Yahweh,
so the people are grass ...

Grass dies, the blossom fades,
but the word of our God will be forever ...

95

2

Yet, Zion says: Yahweh has abandoned me.
My master has forgotten me.

Can a woman forget the baby she feeds?
Her own baby?
Yes. She can forget.
But I will never forget you.

Look! I have engraved you on my palms.
Your walls are forever before me.
Your annihilators will go.
Your sons will hurry back ...
Look round! See them gathered to you.
I swear, they'll cover you like jewels
on your wedding day!
For all your wasteland and ruin
there won't be room enough!
Your enemies will be far gone ...

The children of your exile will whisper in your ear:
There's too little room.
Make room for me to settle.
You'll ask yourself: Am I the mother of all these?
Am I not bereaved, exiled, miserable?
Who bore me these? For I was left alone,
and these − where are they from?

This is my reply:

I will lift my hand, raise my banner
to all nations.
They will carry your sons in their arms,
and your daughters on their shoulders ...
Kings will foster you.
Queens will feed you at the breast,
bow to you, lick the dust of your feet.
And you will know that I am Yahweh.
Those who trust me will not be put to shame!

3

Where is your mother's bill of divorce
showing I sent her away?
Which of my creditors can say

that I sold out to him?
You sold out when you sinned.
Your rebellions exiled her.

When I came, why was no man there?
When I called, why was there no reply?
Is my hand too weak to redeem?
Have I no strength to save?

In my rage I can dry the sea,
I can turn rivers to deserts,
their fish to dry and rot,
I can dress the skies in darkness,
cover them in sackcloth ...

Sing, barren one, childless!
  Break into song, shout aloud!
for the children of exile
    exceed those of marriage!

Widen your tent, stretch the curtains out.
Don't hold back – lengthen the ropes,
            strengthen the pegs ...
You will scatter north and south,
your sons will inherit nations,
and bring empty cities to life.

Do not fear, there's no reason,
it's no season for shame.
You will forget the scandal of your youth,
the disgrace of being a widow:
Your husband is your Maker, Yahweh Zebaot.
Your redeemer – Kedosh Yisrael,
Lord of the earth!

As to a wife, abandoned and grieved,
I call you, wife of my youth, once despised:

I forsook you for a short time,
but I will take you back lovingly.
Though I hid my face in a flash of rage,
my mercy opens to you
in eternal love.

I am the Lord your Redeemer!
                        (From *Isaiah* 40, 49, 50, 54)

97

The Judeans immediately began to rebuild the Temple. They were thwarted at first by the inhabitants of the province of Samaria, who reckoned themselves to be Israelites and demanded a part in the rebuilding of the the Temple. When the Judeans refused to recognize them as Israelites and spurned their offer of help, they took revenge by spreading the calumny that the Jews intended to rebel against the Persians. Work on the Temple was halted even before Cyrus's death in 530 and, after periodic delays, the building was not completed until the reign of Darius I, in 515.

Yet, despite the political and economic hardships faced by the Judeans in re-establishing themselves, some were highly motivated. Undoubtedly they felt that their people had barely escaped spiritual as well as physical extinction. Though few in number, they kept alive the hope that the rest of the exiles would someday follow them.

However, exile in Babylonia had deeply affected the Judean conception of Yahweh and their own role in history. The universalist element which had existed previously in Yahweh worship now became especially pronounced as the Jews became more cosmopolitan. To an extent, this was a natural result of their contact with a wide assortment of peoples in the Babylonian empire. But it might also have included a compensatory quality: if the Judeans no longer had control over their own country, their God was still God of the whole earth. Cyrus's edict of liberation appeared to confirm this view of Yahweh.

However, the evolution of Yahweh from being a purely national, territorial God to being the Master of the Universe inevitably brought with it a paradox: Judah was both unlike and like other nations. Yahweh's power was not confined to Judah, and Judean beliefs and hopes were far from unique. Jeremiah, for example, reportedly predicted that the Judean exile would last seventy years (25:11–12; 29:10), but at least five other defeated or exiled nations are also given hope by the prophets of Yahweh, including one, Phoenicia, whose restoration after defeat by the Assyrians (c. 722, though this passage almost certainly refers to a later period) was due to take place seventy years later (*Isaiah* 23:17). Jeremiah also predicted (assuming that these prophecies were not interpolated) the revival of the Transjordanian kingdoms of Moab (48:47) and Ammon (49:6), and of Elam, east of Mesopotamia (49:39). Ezekiel, similarly, predicted that the restoration of Egypt would take place forty years after its defeat by the Babylonians (29:13).

If Yahweh was God of the nations, what role did Judah play in history? The answer is given in the following poem by Second Isaiah: Judah's redemption was part of the redemption of all nations (which,

in a literal sense, it was). The image of the suffering servant is an
idealized, poetic portrait of the nation in exile, though it might not be
that alone.

THE SUFFERING SERVANT

Yahweh called me from my mother's womb,
he sharpened my tongue like a sword.
He hid me in the shadow of his hand –
a straight arrow in his quiver.
He said: You are my servant, Israel,
to bring me glory!

And I said: I have slaved for nothing,
spent my strength in vain.
But let Yahweh judge me
and what I have done.

Now he means to bring Israel back
(but they won't be gathered!).
Yahweh will honour me so,
for he was my strength!

He says: It is not enough you are my servant,
not enough to restore the tribes of Israel,
or to bring the survivors back –

I have made you a light of salvation
to all peoples!

Thus, Yahweh, Holy One, Redeemer of Israel –
to a people utterly despised,
slaves of the mighty!

(– Kings will rise, princes will bow,
for Yahweh was true to Israel:
And he chose you!)

He says: My servant will rise
to the highest success, astonishing
as his ruin.
(Why, then he hardly looked human!)
Nations will be dazzled, kings struck dumb:
'Who could have thought it possible?

To whom is Yahweh's power shown?
He looked like nothing, formless as a plant
poking up in the desert,
despised, grief-stricken, marked with illness ...
Men turned their eyes away.
We thought he was plagued, tormented, stricken by Yahweh.
Yet, he bore our sickness, suffered our pain.
He was the victim of our sins.
We were healed because he suffered ...'

Now, Israel, my servant, chosen one,
descendant of Abraham my beloved,
whom I have gathered from the ends of the earth,
saying: You are my servant.
I have chosen you. I do not despise you –
Do not be afraid worm-Jacob, people of Israel.
This is what I have done:

I have made you strong as a thresher,
brand new, full of teeth
to thresh mountains, crush them,
turn hills to straw.
You'll toss them in the winnow,
the wind will carry them off,
a storm will scatter them –

And you will rejoice in Yahweh,
praise Kedosh Yisrael!

(from Isaiah 41, 49, 53)

The missionary cause of Judaism – of the universal God of truth and justice, the roots of which may be discerned already in *Jeremiah* (10:11) – gradually became as pervasive, complex and ambiguous as the concept of imperialism which had influenced it, perhaps decisively. It could act as a form of revenge upon or identification with the aggressor, or a beacon of faith and humanitarianism; a triumphant statement of having survived; a gesture of violence or arrogance; an attack on human foibles; an outlet for bitterness built up over two centuries of defeat, repression and exile; and, not least, as an enthusiastic wish to share with humanity what had been learned from bitter experience. Initially, under the impact of defeat, the vengeful motives might well have predominated. Horrific curses against the nations, in the book of Jeremiah (10:25) and in the Psalms (137:7–9), date from the exile. The idea of a universal God ruling all nations, with Israel as his Chosen People, 'a light to the nations', clearly involved at first an attack on the *raison d'être* of imperialism. Likewise, the idea that the nations were *obliged* to recognize the true God and would be punished if they refused, was part of the howl of outrage and grief following the downfall of Judah. The hope for the 'conversion' of the pagans was, similarly, a product of a national psychology deeply scarred by defeat, in need of approval and revitalization; the ideal of a worldwide religion was good for morale and offered a symbolic victory over Judah's oppressors. And the fierce attacks on idols and idol-worship as the soul of stupidity was, at the time, a blow of the powerless and the defeated against the faith of empires.

In Second Isaiah in particular, the anger and frustration suppressed in exile among the people who had defeated and exiled Judah, seems to have found an outlet in the assault on idols. The prophet conveniently overlooks the irony that the Persians, Judah's saviours, were themselves fervent idol-worshippers and that Cyrus, Judah's 'messiah', worshipped the Babylonian gods Bel (Marduk) and Nebo as authors of his victories and described himself as one 'whose rule Bel and Nebo love, whom they want as king to please their hearts' (Pritchard, p. 316). The 2,000-year-old Mesopotamian kingdoms had ended, their gods (Bel, Nebo, etc.) had failed them and were carried off by the victors. This fate, of course, could not befall the invisible God of the universe, an argument which was, no doubt, used by some faithful Judeans concerned by the depletion of their numbers to encourage (perhaps frighten) the pagans to adopt Judaism. Thus, apparently for the first time, a primitive form of 'conversion' developed, which became increasingly sophisticated in coming centuries.

THE STUPIDITY OF IDOLATRY

To whom can you compare God?
What image can you make of him?

One made by a craftsman?
Gold-laid by a goldsmith?
Silver-chained by a silversmith?

Or something downmarket,
of unrotted wood, well-crafted,
so it won't fall down? . . .

Idolmakers are tohu-
their precious works do no good,
the worshippers do not see, do not know
to be ashamed ...

Who in his right mind
would make a god, melt an image –
useless?

His friends should be embarrassed,
crimson-faced craftsmen huddled together
should fear for him and be ashamed.

The smith makes a good job of it,
he works it over the coals
   shapes it with hammers
using his muscles –
when he's hungry he can't go on,
thirst makes him tired ...

The carpenter measures,
marks it with pencil, plans it
   with compass and plane –
makes it in a man's image, a glorious man
to sit at home!

He cuts trees down,
cedars, oaks, pines, well-watered,
used for timber, for heat,
for baking bread –
and for making gods
to kneel and pray to and worship,
half the tree for the roast
('Ah! I'm warm now, it's light inside!')
the other half a deity
('Save me! You are my god!').

*   *   *

Bel is bowed, Nebo bent double –
a heavy load of gods
carried by weary beasts

Figure 16 Ram-headed god of wood, Thebes, *c.* 1320

buckling under the weight –
They did not save a soul,
exiles all ...

Listen to me, house of Jacob,
survivors of the house of Israel!

I carry you from the womb
from birth through life
till old age, I am constant –
I made you and I will carry you
and I will suffer you
and save you ...

(from *Isaiah* 40, 44, 46)

The last prophets hoped for the restoration of the exiles and of the Temple, and for the re-establishment of the Davidic dynasty and of Judah as an independent power, 'strong as a thresher', in the words of Second Isaiah (41:15). None of these aims was fully achieved: the exiles did not return *en masse*; the new Temple was a disappointment in comparison with the magnificent Temple of Solomon; and the Davidic kingdom was not renewed. Yet, there were hopes that Zerubbabel, or a descendant of his might, at the end of days, become the Messiah, king of a new Judean state. The death of Cyrus's son, Cambyses, around 522, the unrest within the Persian empire which followed and the revolt of the Babylonians nourished the Judean hopes for a revived independent monarchy under Zerubbabel. However, the Persian empire survived under Darius I, and Zerubbabel mysteriously disappeared from history after the completion of the Temple. But the messianic hope was kindled, and is epitomized in the following lines with their anti-imperialist, pacifist thrust from the book of Zechariah.

THE MESSIAH

Shout for joy, daughter of Zion,
    daughter of Jerusalem!
Your king comes for you in triumph,
a poor man, riding on a donkey,
    a plain he-donkey –
for I will ban the chariot in Ephraim,
and the warhorse in Jerusalem –
I will break the bow of battle ...

He will talk peace with the nations,
his rule from sea to sea, from the Euphrates
to the world's end ...
And for you, too – for your covenant's
blood –
I loosed your captives from the parched pit:

Return to the fortress – Jerusalem,
O prisoners of hope! ...

(*Zechariah* 9:9–12)

On a note of frustration and guarded hope, the prophetic age ended. The anxieties and uncertainties which often underlie the need for a Messiah also drew the prophets to speculation on the apocalyptic end of days, when God would defeat Israel's enemies, judge the nations and bring a golden age of peace to mankind. With the fall of Judah, its centuries-old monarchy going back to David had vanished. In mourning their lost kingdom, the Judeans were drawn more strongly than ever before to the anthropomorphic concept of the kingdom of God and of God as the true and ultimate imperial conqueror. This perception of God might be seen as an ironic survival of the Mesopotamian empires. In the spiritual realm, the prophets gained the total victory denied to the Judeans by their mere survival. Poetry was the instrument of this victory. It was, and remains, a means of ensuring the survival of Judaism. It offered, and still offers, inspiration to mankind. Not least, it was, and still is, a source of immense aesthetic pleasure, as unique, finely-wrought art.

Figure 17   Assyrian king fighting lions, possibly symbolic of his enemies, *c.* 645

ON THE WARPATH

North from Teman, Eloah will come,
past Paran, the Holy One.
His glory wraps the skies,
the earth is filled with his praise.
Horns of light, hidden strength,
bursting from his hands.
Plague scorches his way.
Fire bolts at his feet.

He stops – the earth shudders.
A glance – nations tremble.
Timeless mountains crumble.
Hills bow ancient heads.
He follows their eternal paths.
I see tents of Cushan terrified,
Midianite curtains shake.

Does your fury parch rivers,
Yahweh! Is your rage against the rivers?
Is your wrath against the sea? –
You ride your horses, with naked bow
on the chariot of victory!
Seven sea-beds cleft with your word,
you furrow the earth with rivers.

Mountains rumble at the sight of you.
Deluge follows – Tehom roars,
hands stretched out!
Sun and moon – petrified
by the flash of your arrows,
the lightning of your spear.

You stamp the earth in rage
in anger thresh nations.
You come to save your people,
to rescue your anointed.
You decapitate the house of the wicked,
cutting its neck bare to the base.
You pierce the heads of their rulers
with their own weapons
as they storm in to scatter us,
happy to devour the poor, in secret.
You tread the sea with your horses,
mightily the waters foamed!

When I heard, I quaked inside.
My lips trembled.

If I wait careless for the day of calamity,
for our marauding foes,
let rottenness ravage my bones,
let the earth shake beneath me!

Though the fig-tree blossom not,
the vine be empty of grapes,
though the olives rot on the branch,
and the fertile earth yields no fruit,
though the sheep are cut from the fold,
and no cattle stand in the stall –

Yet in Yahweh will I exult,
rejoice in the God who saves me.

Yahweh my master gives me strength.
He makes my feet swift as a hind,
and guides me across the high mountains.

(*Habakkuk* 3:3–19)

THE DAY OF JUDGEMENT

Proclaim it among the nations:
Get ready for war!
Alert the warriors!
Beat your ploughshares into swords,
    pruning-hooks into spears!
Even weaklings will bear them!

Gather quickly, nations!
Bring your fighters, Yahweh!
To the valley of Jehoshafat:
There I will sit and judge
all nations.

The harvest is ripe for the sickle –
Wield it!
The vats overflow with grapes –
Tread them!
For there is much wickedness!

Multitudes, multitudes, in the valley
of decision. The day of Yahweh is near!
Sun and moon turn black.
Stars do not shine.

Out of Zion and Jerusalem
Yahweh roars,
shaking heaven and earth ...

Yet, he is his people's shelter,
fortress to the children of Israel –

So you shall know:
I am Yahweh your God, dweller in Zion,
my holy mountain –
Jerusalem will be holy.
No invader will trample it again ...

Judah will be forever,
Jerusalem, generation after generation,
inhabited.
I'll wipe the bloody slate clean,
for Yahweh is in Zion!

(Joel 4:9–17, 20–1)

BIBLIOGRAPHY

I TRANSLATIONS

The following are a few of the best-known English translations of the Bible. In addition, many of the commentaries and editions in the next section include new translations, with variant readings.

The Holy Bible, an interlinear edition containing the 1611 King James translation as well as the RSV, London: Cambridge University Press, 1906.

The Holy Bible, Revised Standard Version, London: Nelson, 1952 (first published 1881–4).

The Holy Scriptures According to the Masoretic Text, Philadelphia: Jewish Publication Society of America, 1947 (first published 1917).

The New English Bible: The Old Testament, ed. chairman Donald Ebor, Oxford: Oxford University Press, Cambridge: Cambridge University Press, 1970.

A New Translation of the Bible, tr. James Moffat, London: Hodder & Stoughton, 1929.

The Revised English Bible with the Apocrypha, Oxford: Oxford University Press, Cambridge: Cambridge University Press, 1989.

Tanakh: The Holy Scriptures: The New JPS Translation According to the Traditional Hebrew Text, Philadelphia, New York: Jewish Publication Society of America, 1985.

II EDITIONS AND COMMENTARIES

While a number of important editions and commentaries, such as the *International Critical Commentary* and Kittel's *Biblica Hebraica*, appeared before World War II, there has been a flood of critical literature since the war. This work is often repetitive and of uneven quality, though among the most highly regarded are *The Interpreter's Bible* and *The Anchor Bible*, being readable, reliable and accessible.

The Anchor Bible, 44 vols, ed. William Foxwell Albright and David Noel Freedman, Garden City, New York: Doubleday & Co., 1964–77.

The Cambridge Bible Commentary, 53 vols, ed. P.R. Ackroyd, A.R.C. Leaney and J.W. Packer, Cambridge: Cambridge University Press, 1965–79.

The Expositor's Bible Commentary, 12 vols, ed. Frank E. Gaebelein, Grand Rapids, Michigan: Zondervan Publishing House, 1979–81.

The International Critical Commentary on The Holy Scriptures of the Old and New Testaments, 47 vols, ed. Samuel Rolles Driver, Alfred Plummer and Charles Augustus Briggs, Edinburgh: T. & T. Clark, 1910–20.

The Interpreter's Bible, 12 vols, ed. George Arthur Buttrick *et al.*, New York and Nashville: Abingdon Cokesbury Press, 1952–7.

The Interpreter's Dictionary of the Bible: An Illustrated Encyclopedia, 4 vols, ed. George Arthur Buttrick *et al.*, New York and Nashville: Abingdon Press, 1962. Supplementary volume, general ed. Keith Crim, 1976.

The Interpreter's One-Volume Commentary on The Bible, ed. Charles M. Layman, London and Glasgow: Collins, 1972.

New Century Bible, 31 vols, general eds Ronald E. Clements and Matthew Black, London: Oliphants, 1966–92.

The New International Commentary on the Old Testament, ed. R.K. Harrison, Grand Rapids, Michigan: William B. Eerdmans Publishing Company, 1965–90.

The New Jerome Biblical Commentary, ed. R.E. Brown, J.A. Fitzmyer and R.E. Murphy, London: G. Chapman, 1990.

The New Jerusalem Bible, general ed. Henry Wansbrough, London: Darton, Longman & Todd, 1985.

Peake's Commentary on the Bible, ed. Matthew Black and H.H. Rowley, London: Thomas Nelson and Sons Ltd, 1962.

The Soncino Books of the Bible, 14 vols, ed. A. Cohen, London and Bournemouth: Soncino Press, 1945–52. Includes, among other things, useful synopses in English of medieval Hebrew commentaries.

Torch Bible Commentaries, 43 vols, ed. John Marsh, Alan Richardson and R. Gregor Smith, London: SCM Press, 1949–73.

Tyndale Old Testament Commentaries, general ed. D.J. Wiseman, London: Tyndale Press, 1967–72.

Westminster Commentaries, 56 vols, ed. Walter Lock and D.C. Simpson, London: Methuen, 1904–34.

World Biblical Commentary, 51 vols, ed. David A. Hubbard and Glenn W. Barker, Waco, Texas: Word Book, Publisher, 1984–7.

III THE PROPHETS

Anderson, Bernhard W., *The Eighth Century Prophets*, London: SPCK, 1979.

Anderson, Bernhard W. and Harrelson, Walter, *Israel's Prophetic Heritage*, essays in honour of James Muilenberg, New York: Harper & Brothers, 1962.

Bewer, Julius A. (ed.), *The Prophets*, New York: Harper & Brothers Publishers, London: Eyre and Spottiswoode Ltd, 1949.

Blenkinsopp, J.A., *A History of Prophecy in Israel: From the Settlement in the Land to the Hellenistic Period*, London: SPCK, 1984.

Carroll, Robert P., *When Prophecy Failed: Cognitive Dissonance in the Prophetic Tradition of the Old Testament*, New York: The Seabury Press, 1979.

Childs, Brevard S., *Isaiah and the Assyrian Crisis*, London: SCM Press, 1967.

Clements, R.E., *Prophecy and Tradition*, Atlanta, Georgia: John Knox Press, 1975.
—— R.E., *Isaiah and the Deliverance of Jerusalem*, Sheffield: JSOT Press, 1980.
Coggins, R., Phillips, A. and Knibb, M. (eds), *Israel's Prophetic Tradition*, essays in honour of Peter R. Ackroyd, Cambridge: Cambridge University Press, 1982.
Crenshaw, James L., *Prophetic Conflict: Its Effects Upon Israelite Religion*, Berlin and New York: Walter de Gruyter, 1971.
Geller, Stephen A., 'Were the prophets poets?' *Prooftexts* 3 (1983) 211–21.
Heaton, E.W., *The Old Testament Prophets*, Harmondsworth: Penguin, 1958.
Henshaw, T., *The Latter Prophets*, London: Allen & Unwin, 1958.
Heschel, Abraham J., *The Prophets*, New York: Jewish Publication Society, 1962.
Koch, Klaus, *The Prophets*, 2 vols, tr. M. Kohl, London: SCM Press, 1982, 1983.
Lindblom, J., *Prophecy in Ancient Israel*, Philadelphia: Fortress Press, 1962.
Liwak, R., *Der Prophet und die Geschichte*, Stuttgart: Verlag W. Kohlhammer, 1987.
Lods, A., *The Prophets and the Rise of Judaism*, London: Kegan Paul, 1937.
Mays, James L. and Achtemeier, Paul J. (eds), *Interpreting the Prophets*, Philadelphia: Fortress Press, 1987.
Petersen, David L. (ed.), *Prophecy in Israel*, London: SPCK, Philadelphia: Fortress Press, 1987.
Rowley, H.H., *Men of God: Studies in Old Testament History and Prophecy*, Edinburgh: Thomas Nelson & Sons, 1963.
Sawyer, J.F.A., *Prophecy and the Prophets of the Old Testament*, Oxford: The Oxford Bible Series, 1987.
Schofield, J.N., *Law, Prophets and Writings*, London: SPCK, 1969.
Whitley, C.F., *The Prophetic Achievement*, London: A.R. Mowbray, 1963.
Wilson, Robert R., *Prophecy and Society in Ancient Israel*, Philadelphia: Fortress Press, 1980.

IV   THE HEBREW BIBLE AND THE ANCIENT NEAR EAST

Albright, William Foxwell, *Archaeology and the Religion of Israel*, Garden City, New York: Anchor Books, 1969 (first published 1943).
Anderson, Bernhard W., *The Living World of The Old Testament*, 2nd edn, London: Longman, 1973.
Barnett, R.D., *Assyrian Palace Reliefs and their Influence on the Sculpture of Babylonia and Persia*, photographs by W. Forman, London: Batchworth, n.d.
—— *Assyrian Sculpture in the British Museum*, photographs by A. Lorenzini, Toronto: McLelland & Stewart, 1975.
Barton, J., *Oracles of God: Perceptions of Ancient Prophecy in Israel after the Exile*, London: Darton, Longman & Todd, 1986.
Boardman, J. *et al.* (eds), *The Cambridge Ancient History*, vol. III, pt 2, *The Assyrian and Babylonian Empires and other States of the Near East, from the Eighth to the Sixth Centuries B.C.*, Cambridge: Cambridge University Press, 1991. Bibliography on pp. 755–819.
Davies, W.D. and Finkelstein, Louis (eds), *The Cambridge History of Judaism:*

Introduction: The Persian Period, Cambridge: Cambridge University Press, 1984. Includes bibliography on prophecy in the Persian period, pp. 427–30.

Douglas, J.D. (organizing ed.), *The Illustrated Bible Dictionary*, 3 vols, Sydney and Auckland: Inter-Varsity Press, Tynedale House Publishers and Hodder & Stoughton, 1980.

The Epic of Gilgamesh, tr. N.K. Sanders, Harmondsworth: Penguin, 1960.

Garbini, Giovanni, *History and Ideology in Ancient Israel*, tr. John Bowden, New York: Crossroad, 1988.

Gaster, Theodor H., *Myth, Legend and Custom in The Old Testament*, London: Duckworth, 1969.

Grant, Michael, *The History of Ancient Israel*, London: Weidenfeld & Nicolson, 1984.

Hayes, John H. and Miller, J. Maxwell (eds), *Israelite and Judean History*, Philadelphia: Westminster Press, 1977.

Kaufmann, Yehezkel, *History of the Religion of Israel*, 4 vols, tr. M. Greenberg, New York: Union of American Hebrew Congregations, 1970.

Kermode, Frank and Alter, Robert (eds), *The Literary Guide to the Bible*, Cambridge, Mass.: Belknap Press of Harvard University Press, 1987.

McNutt, Paula M., *The Forging of Israel: Iron Technology, Symbolism and Tradition in Ancient Society*, Sheffield: Almond Press, 1990.

Noth, Martin, *The Old Testament World*, tr. Victor I. Gruhn, London: A. & C. Black, 1966.

Orlinsky, Harry M., *Ancient Israel*, Ithaca, New York: Cornell University Press, 1954.

Pritchard, James B., *Ancient Near Eastern Texts Relating to the Old Testament*, 3rd edn, Princeton: Princeton University Press, 1969.

Rad, Gerhard von, *Old Testament Theology*, 2 vols, tr. D.M.G. Stalker, London: SCM Press, 1975 (first published 1957).

Rowley, H.H. (ed.), *The Old Testament in Modern Study*, Oxford: Oxford University Press, 1961 (first published 1951). Contains a wide bibliographic summary on 'The prophetic literature' by Otto Eissfeldt, pp. 115–61.

Saggs, H.W., *The Greatness that was Babylon*, London: Sidgwick & Jackson, 1962.

——*Everyday Life in Babylonia and Assyria*, London: B.T. Batsford Ltd, New York: G.P. Putnam's Sons, 1965.

——*The Might That Was Assyria*, London: Sidgwick & Jackson, 1984.

Thomas, D. Winton (ed.), *Documents from Old Testament Times*, London: Thomas Nelson & Sons, 1958.

Thompson, Michael E.W., *Situation and Theology: Old Testament Interpretation of the Syro-Ephraimite War, CA. 734*, Sheffield: Almond Press, 1982.

Wiseman, D.J., *Nebuchadrezzar and Babylon*, Oxford: Oxford University Press, 1985.

Wright, G. Ernest (ed.), *The Bible and the Ancient Near East*, essays in honour of William Foxwell Albright, London: Routledge & Kegan Paul, 1961.

Yadin, Yigael, *The Art of Warfare in Biblical Lands in the Light of Archaeological Study*, 2 vols, New York: McGraw-Hill, 1963.

V IMPERIALISM

There is a large and growing literature on imperialism and the following gives no more than a rough idea of some of the main authors, texts and currents of thought. Included are a number of readers which give useful introductions, extracts and bibliography on modern as well as ancient imperialism. However, there is surprisingly little devoted specifically to Mesopotamian imperialism in the time of the prophets.

Boulding, Kenneth, E. and Mukerjee, Tapan, *Economic Imperialism: A Book of Readings*, Ann Arbor: University of Michigan Press, 1972.

Cogan, Morton, *Imperialism and Religion: Assyria, Judah and Israel in the Eighth and Seventh Centuries B.C.E.*, Missoula, Montana: Society of Biblical Literature and Scholars Press, 1974.

Doyle, Michael W., *Empires*, Ithaca, New York: Cornell University Press, 1986.

Fieldhouse, D.K., *The Theory of Capitalist Imperialism*, London: Longman, 1967.

Garnsey, P.D.A. and Whittaker, C.R. (eds), *Imperialism in the Ancient World*, Cambridge: Cambridge University Press, 1978.

Harris, William V., *War and Imperialism in Republican Rome 327–70 B.C.*, Oxford: Clarendon Press, 1985.

Hobsbawm, E.J., *The Age of Empire 1875–1914*, London: Weidenfeld & Nicolson, 1987.

Hobson, J., *Imperialism: A Study*, London: Allen & Unwin, 1938 (first published 1902).

Kiernan, V.G., *Marxism and Imperialism*, London: Edward Arnold, 1974.

Lichtheim, George, *Imperialism*, Harmondsworth: Penguin, 1971.

Mack, Andrew, Plant, David and Doyle, Ursula (eds), *Imperialism: Intervention and Development*, London: Croom Helm, 1979.

Mommsen, Wolfgang J., *Theories of Imperialism*, London: Weidenfeld & Nicolson, 1980.

Mommsen, Wolfgang J. and Osterhammel, Jürgen (eds), *Imperialism and After*, The German Historical Institute, London: Allen & Unwin, 1986.

Owen, R. and Sutcliffe, B. (eds), *Studies in the Theory of Imperialism*, London: Longman, 1972.

Schumpeter, Joseph A., *Imperialism and Social Classes*, ed. Paul M. Sweezy, tr. Heinz Norden, Oxford: Blackwell, 1951.

Snyder, Louis, L., *The Imperialist Reader*, Port Washington, New York, London: Kennikat Press, 1973.

Weber, Max, *General Economic History*, tr. Frank H. Knight, New York: Collier Books, 1961 (first published 1923).

INDEX

Numbers in italics signify a biblical text.

Ahaz: Aram, adoption of cultic practices 26–7, 33; Assyrian vassal-king
26–7, 35; and child-sacrifice 26;
death (720) 35–6; Hezekiah, son of
Ahaz 45; Isaiah, ignores advice of
26; Israel, war with 22, *29* (Isaiah
ben Amoz), 35; Judah, king of at
time of fall of Israel (721) 33; Manasseh, grandson of Ahaz 53; Mesopotamian inscriptions, mentioned
in 3
Akkadian 2
Ammon 1, 63, 98
Amos 5, 11, 20, *21–2*
Arabia: prophecy of Isaiah ben Amoz
5, 34, 37, *38*
Aram: Assyria, wars against 20; Isaiah
ben Amoz, prophecy of 5, *27,
29*; Judah, attacks on instigated
by Babylonia 63; Aram and
Israel: allied in war against
Judah and Assyria 26, *29*, 35;
proximity 2; Israel repopulated
by Arameans after exile (721)
33
Ashurbanipal: death 10, 12, 54;
success in maintaining Assyrian
empire 7
Asshur 2
Assyria: Arabia, conquest of 37; army
8, 23; Babylonia, wars with 10,
26, 33–4, 38, 42, *43–4* (Isaiah ben
Amoz), 45; causes of fall 6, 54,
55; civilization, importance of in
survival 8; culture 2, 10, 42; deportation of defeated enemies 5–6, 33,
50, 51–2, 65, 92; 'died of indigestion' 10; Egypt, conquest of 38,
39–40 (Isaiah ben Amoz), 74; Elam,
wars with 33, 42, 61, 92; Ethiopia,
conquest of *40–1* (Isaiah ben
Amoz), 74; and 'ethnic cleansing'
xi; expansionism, motives for 6–7;
fall and disappearance of 2, 6, 10,
12, 13, *46* (Isaiah ben Amoz), 54,
55ff.; Jerusalem, siege of by Sennacherib (701) 42, 46ff.; Israel's
exile to *23–6* (Hosea); Judah,
alliance with against Israel and
Aram (8th century) 26–7, *28–9*
(Isaiah ben Amoz); lions, mortally
wounded as symbols of empire 14;
locusts, compared to plague of 62;
military campaigns 5–6, 26–7, 33–
4, 68; Moab, conquest of 36; power
of 2; and prophecy 1, 2, 16; religion
2, 7, 10, 11, 42; revolts against 10,
33–4, 45; rod of Yahweh's wrath *29*
(Isaiah ben Amoz); Tyre, conquest
of 34; tyrant 2, 3, 10, 33, 42, *56–8*
(Nahum); and use of iron 8; violence
of and biblical world 3; 'will fall by
no man's sword' 46; *see also* Fertile
Crescent; imperialism; Nahum;
Nineveh; prophets and prophecy,
art of

Assyria and prophecies of Isaiah ben Amoz 5, *29*, 42; rarely mentioned 34, 39, 81; Assyria 'rod of my wrath' 2, 12, 20, *29*, 47

Babylon: Assyria, defeats by 42; Cyrus, conquest by (539) 12, 50, 89–90, *90–1* (Jeremiah); Isaiah ben Amoz, prophecy against *43–4*; Jehoiachin in exile 65, 66, 87, 89; Jeremiah on fall of (539) *90–1*; Judah a vassal of 62; Judeans in 87; Judean lion exiled to *67* (Ezekiel); site, forgotten 2, excavations of 87; *see also* Babylonia

Babylonia: Assyria, rivalry and wars with 10, 26, 33–4, 38, 42, *43–4* (Isaiah ben Amoz), 45, 54, 55; culture 2, 42; in Ezekiel's prophecies to Tyre? 81; Egypt, rivalry and wars with 12, 58, *60–1* (Jeremiah), 62, 63; fall and disappearance (539) 2, 12, 13, 89–90, *90–1* (Jeremiah); Isaiah ben Amoz's prophecy 5, 34, *43–4*; Judah, invasion and conquest of 69–81; Judean exiles in 70, 87, 89, 92–3; Judean exiles return from 93, *95–7* (Second Isaiah), 98; and prophecy 1, 2; religion of 2, 7, 42, 101, *102* (Second Isaiah); revolt against Persia 104; *see also* Babylon, Nebuchadrezzar

Calah 2
Cambyses 104
Carchemish, battle of (605) 12, 15, 60, *60–1* (Jeremiah), 68
Chaldea 63, *90* (Jeremiah)
child-sacrifice 26, *33* (Micah), 54
Cyrus II: Babylonia, conquest of (539) 12, 50, 89–90; Edict of Return 12, 91–2, 98–9; enlightened form of imperialism 91–2; as Judah's 'messiah' 92, *93–5* (Second Isaiah), 101; restoration of sacred objects of Temple 92

Damascus *27* (Isaiah ben Amoz)
Darius I 98

Deborah 2, *3*, 58
Dumah 37

Edom (= Seir): adjacent to Judah 2; invasion of Judean territory 35, 78, *79–81* (Obadiah); Isaiah's prophecy to 5; Jeremiah's prophecy to 42; 'A voice calls me from Seir' 38
Egypt: Assyria, rivalry and wars with 2, 7, 10, 26, 33, 38, *39–40* (Isaiah ben Amoz), 53–4, 74; Babylonia, rivalry and wars with 12, 58, *60–1* (Jeremiah), 62, 63; Carchemish, defeat at by Babylonia (605) 12, 15, *60–1* (Jeremiah), 68; crocodile *68–9* (Ezekiel); and prophecies of Ezekiel *68–9*, 74, 98; and prophecies of Isaiah ben Amoz 5, 34, *39–40*, 42, *45*; and prophecies of Jeremiah *60–1*; trade with Tyre *34* (Isaiah ben Amoz), *83* (Ezekiel)
Egypt and Israel: exiled population of *24* (Hosea), *26* (Hosea), *67* (Ezekiel); exodus of Israel *50* (Hosea), *51*, (Isaiah ben Amoz), 68, *69* (Ezekiel)
Egypt and Judah: alliances 45, 68, 77; exiled population of Judah 78; Egyptian victory at Megiddo (609) 12, 58
Ekron 46
Elam 33, 42, 61, 92, 98
Elijah 20
Elisha 20
Ephraim *see* Israel
Epic of Gilgamesh 14
Esarhaddon: death of 10; success in maintaining Assyrian empire 7
Ethiopia: 'are you different from the Ethiopians, children of Israel?' 22; prophecies of Isaiah ben Amoz 5, 34, *40–1*, 74
Evil-Merodach 89
Ezekiel: appeasement, message of 66; Babylonia, exile to in 597 66; Babylonian empire, leading prophet in 1; catastrophic events, 'acting out' of 74, *75–7*; compared with Jeremiah 70, 73–4; dating, precision in 15; dry bones, prophecy

Ezekiel—*cont.*
of 74, *88–9*; Egypt, prophecies concerning *68–9*, 74, 98; exile, only known prophet who prophesied in 74; on harlotry of Israel 74; Hosea, influence of 74; Isaiah ben Amoz, influence of 74; Jeremiah, contemporary of 66; Jerusalem, siege of *75–7*; Judah, allegory of lions 15, *66–7*; priest 66; prophecies to the nations 5, *68–9*, 74, *81–5*; theophany 74; Tyre, prophecies against *81–5*; warnings ignored 77; wife, death of symbolic of destruction of Temple 74, *77*

Fertile Crescent: Assyrian conquest of xiv, 2, 5, 35, 53–4; Babylonian conquest of 55ff., 62; Persian conquest of 89–90

Gath 21
Gedaliah 78

Habakkuk *59, 105–7*
Haggai 32
Hamath 21, 22
Hebrew 2, 14, 74–5
Hezekiah: advised by Isaiah, to avoid revolt against Assyria 45, to resist Assyrian siege of Jerusalem (701) 47; Ahaz's son 45; builds conduit from stream of Gihon to Jerusalem 9; Manasseh's father 53; Mesopotamian inscriptions, mentioned in 3; religious reforms 45; trapped 'like a bird in a cage' 46
Hosea: Assyria, no 'burden of Asshur' in prophecies 11; children 23; Israel, as whore, depiction of *23–6*, 70, 74; Jeremiah, influence on 70; marriage to whore 23; only prophet of Israel? 20; written prophecy, author of some of the earliest surviving 5, 20
Hoshea 26

idols and idol-worship: Ahaz, adoption of Aramean cultic practices 26–7; Egypt, idol-worship to stave off Assyrians *39* (Isaiah ben Amoz); Josiah's abolition of 54, *54–5* (Zephaniah); Manasseh's adoption of pagan gods and customs 53; prophets' opposition to: Isaiah ben Amoz, prediction of Israel's rejection of idols *46*, Israel, worship of idols 24 (Hosea), Judah, idol-worship enraging Yahweh *72* (Jeremiah), 'paltry polytheism' of Mesopotamia, hatred of 11, in Second Isaiah *101–3*, smith as idol-maker, vituperation of *102*; in 'Song of Moses' 3–4; total rejection of idols 13
imperialism: bibliography on 113; definition and theories of 6ff.; enlightened form of, created by Cyrus II 91; failure of 1, 14, 49, 54, 55, 105; proselytization compared to 13; *see also* Assyria, Babylonia, Iron Age, Judaism, Persia, Yahweh
imperialism and prophets: defence against 8–10; reaction against 1, 44ff., 50–1, 101–2; victory over 1, 105; view of as tool of Yahweh's power, Assyria, rod of Yahweh's wrath 2, 12, 20, *29* (Isaiah ben Amoz), Babylonia, Yahweh's punitive agent 70, Yahweh's avenger against Egypt *60–1*, Persia, Yahweh's shatterer of Babylonia *90* (Jeremiah)
imperialism and war: battles and sieges, Babylon *43* (Isaiah ben Amoz), *90–1* (Jeremiah), Carchemish *60–1* (Jeremiah), Jerusalem 12, 42, 46ff., *63–5* (Jeremiah), 66, 69, 70, *75–6* (Ezekiel), 77, *81* (Ezekiel), Nineveh, *56–8* (Nahum), Samaria 9, *21–2* (Amos), 23, 33, Tyre *34–5* (Isaiah ben Amoz), *81–5* (Ezekiel); campaigns, Assyrian, late 8th century 5, ch. 1, Babylonian, late 7th, early 6th centuries ch. 2, Persian, mid-6th century ch. 3; Iron Age, impact on 8

Iron Age 8ff.

Isaiah ben Amoz: adviser to Judah's kings, Ahaz 26, Hezekiah 45, 46, 47; Assyria, references to 5, *29*, 42, no 'burden of Asshur' 11, 'rod of my wrath' 2, 12, 20, *29*, Yahweh's iron axe leading to victory of 10; Assyrian empire, leading prophet in 1; authorship in doubt 15; belief that faith is stronger than military force 13; Ezekiel, influence on 74; Mesopotamian inscriptions, not mentioned in 3; prophet, among earliest whose writings have survived 20; *see also* Second Isaiah

Isaiah ben Amoz's prophecies: Arabia 5, 34, 37, *38*; Aram 5, *27*; Babylon *43–4*; Damascus *27*; Edom 5; Egypt *39–40, 45–6*, 68, 74; Ethiopia 5, 34, *40–1*, 74; of golden age of military victory and universal peace 4; Israel 22, 27, *28–31*; Judah *28–31, 46–7*; Moab 5, 34, *36–7*; Philistia 5, *36*; Phoenicia 5, *34–5*; Sennacherib *47–8*, 53; Tyre *34–5*

Israel (= Ephraim, Jacob): Aram, alliance with against Assyria and Judah (8th century) 26–7, *28–31*; Assyrian expansionism, effect on 26; fall of and exile 2, 3, 6, 10–11, 20, *21–2* (Amos/Isaiah ben Amoz), *23–6* (Hosea), *27* (Isaiah ben Amoz), *28–31* (Isaiah ben Amoz), *32–3* (Micah), 33, *43* (Isaiah ben Amoz), 52, 68, 87; Hosea the only Israelite prophet? 20; 'marriage' to Yahweh 23, 31, *50* (Hosea), 95, *96–7* (Second Isaiah); in Mesopotamian inscriptions 3; militancy 10, 33, 42; monotheism 3, rejection of 10, 23; Phoenicia, alliance with (9th century) 19; redemption, prophecies of 42, 50, *51* (Amos/Hosea/Isaiah ben Amoz/Micah), 87, *88* (Jeremiah), *89* (Ezekiel); revolt against Assyria 10, 33; Samarian inhabitants of, refusal of Judah to recognize as Israelites (late 6th century) 98; servant of the Lord *93* (Second Isaiah), *99–100* (Second Isaiah); strategic importance of 7, 27; vassaldom to Assyria 27; as vine *24* (Hosea), *28* (Isaiah); as whore *23* (Hosea) 74; *see also* Judah; Mesopotamian inscriptions; Yahweh

Israel and Judah: Israel's destruction a lesson to Judah 11, 51–2; as 'idealized phantom nation' 51; peace between (9th century) 20; war between (late 8th century) 26–7

Jacob *see* Israel

Jehoahaz 58

Jehoiachin: Babylonia inscriptions, mentioned in 87; Evil-Merodach, freed by (581) 87, 89; exiled to Babylonia (597) 65, 66, 87; Jehoiakim, son of 65; Jeremiah's poem on fate of *65–6*; Judean nationalists, focal point of 68, 87, 89; prisoner in Babylon 87; Sheshbazzar, father of 92; Zerubbabel, grandfather of 93

Jehoiakim 58, 63, 65

Jehu 3, 19, 20, 26

Jeremiah: Babylonia, belief that future of Jews lay in 70; Babylonian empire, leading prophet during 1; belief that faith is stronger than military force 13; as confessional poet 69–70, *70–3*; death 78; exile to Egypt 78; as fortification against invasion 10; hope, message of 70, *87–8*; jailed for pro-Babylonian views 12; Judaism, roots of universality of 100; *Lamentations* attributed to 77; land, purchase of in confidence of exiles' return 70; marriage, avoids to symbolize exile 70; Mesopotamian inscriptions, not mentioned in 3; message of appeasement 66; Nebuchadrezzar, as 'servant' of Yahweh 70; priest 66; wears yoke to symbolize servitude of nations to Babylonia 10, 74

Jeremiah's prophecies: Babylon, on fall of *90–1*; Carchemish, poem on

Jeremiah's prophecies—*cont.*
battle of (605) *60–1*; to the nations 5, 42, 98; on God's injustice *59*; on Jehoiachin's fate *65–6*; Nebuchadrezzar's invasion of Judah *63–6*
Jerusalem (capital of kingdom of Judah): and Day of Yahweh *107–8* (Joel); Hezekiah, water conduit of 9; 'if I forget you' 93; Jews, survival in 2; Judean exiles, return to 12–13, 93, *95* (Second Isaiah); 'my blood on Chaldea' 90; Nebuchadrezzar, conquest by (597, 586) 12, *63–5* (Jeremiah), 66, 69, 70, *75–6* (Ezekiel), 77, *81* (Ezekiel); 'return to the fortress' 104; Sennacherib, siege of (701) 42, 46ff.; Temple, rebuilding of 92, 98, 104; Yahweh, protected by *46* (Isaiah ben Amoz); *108* (Joel); *see also* Judah and Judeans
Job 59, 60, 69
Joel *62–3*
Josiah: apocalyptic atmosphere of reign *54–5* (Zephaniah); defeat and death of 12, 58, 60; prophecy, revival of 53; reforms of 13, 54, 58
Judah and Judeans: alliance with Assyria against Israel and Aram (8th century) 26–7, *28–31* (Isaiah ben Amoz); Assyrian conquests, effect on 26–7; Babylonia, overrun and defeated by 62, 63, *63–5* (Jeremiah), 65; cosmopolitanism 13, 81, 98; Egypt, alliances with *45–6* (Isaiah ben Amoz), 68, *68–9* (Ezekiel), 77; empires, anger at *46–8* (Nahum), *90–1* (Jeremiah), 92–3, 100–1, survival of owing to 8, 91–2; exile, threat of and prophetic creativity 5, 11; fall of and exile 2, 3, 6, 12, 52, 69–81, 87, compared to childbirth *65* (Jeremiah), grief over *77–8* (Lamentations), 92; freedom from Assyria 56; Israel, peace with (9th century) 20; Israel's destruction by Assyria, effect on 11, 51–2; as lion *66–7* (Ezekiel); in Mesopotamian inscriptions 3; military weakness

and susceptibility to prophecy 31–2, 70; Moab, refugees from *36–7* (Isaiah ben Amoz); monotheism of 3, 8, 11, 42, 45, 98, 101; power of, God-given *36* (Isaiah ben Amoz); prophets, majority from 20; religious reforms 45 (Hezekiah), 54 (Josiah); return from Babylonian exile 12–13, *89* (Ezekiel), 93, *95* (Second Isaiah), 98; revolt against Assyria 45; strategic importance of 7, 27; vassaldom to Assyria 19, 20, 33, 35, 53, to Egypt 58, to Babylonia 62; as whore 74; *see also* Israel, Jerusalem, Mesopotamian inscriptions, prophets and prophecy, Yahweh
Judaism: crystallization of in exile 13, 100–1; and deportation of Judeans 5–6; and imperialism 13, 100–1, 105; survival and growth of in Persian empire 12; transformation of by prophets 14, 52; *see also* Yahweh

Khorsabad 2

Lachish 4, 9, 25, 46, 79
Lebanon 43, *47* (Isaiah ben Amoz), *83* (Ezekiel); *see also* Phoenicia
Lydia 89

Malachi xiv
Manasseh 12, 53
Media 54, 55
Megiddo *4* (Song of Deborah), 58
Menahem 26
Merodach Baladan 33–4, 45, 48; *see also* Babylonia, rivalry and wars with Assyria
Mesopotamian inscriptions: Ahaz 3; Black Obelisk of Shalmaneser III 19; Cyrus, as idol-worshipper 101; discoveries of 3; gods of Israel, removed to Assyria by Sargon II 23; Hezekiah, trapped 'like a bird in a cage' 46, tribute to Sennacherib (Taylor Prism) 47; Israel and Aram, Assyrian victories over compared to

Mesopotamian inscriptions—*cont.*
flood or storm 27; Jehoiachin and other Judean exiles 87; Jehu 3, 19; 'king of the whole earth', description of Mesopotamian kings 4; kings of Israel and Judah mentioned but no other biblical character 3; Manasseh as vassal-king of Assyria 53; Moabite Stone 36; prophets' knowledge of 16; Qarkar, battle of (c. 853) 20
Micah 5, 11, 15, 20, *32–3*, 70
Midian 62
Moab: Assyria, defeat by (end 8th century) 36; Balak, king of *32* (Micah); Isaiah ben Amoz, prophecies to 5, 34, *36–7*; Jeremiah, prediction of revival of 98; Moabite Stone 36
Moab and Judah: adjacent 2; attacks instigated by Nebuchadrezzar 63; culture similar 36
Moses 3, *32* (Micah)

Nabonidus 89
Nahum 12, 15, 55, *56–8*
Nebuchadrezzar: Carchemish, victorious in battle of (605) 12, 15, 60, *60–1* (Jeremiah) 68; death (562) 87, 89; Egypt, campaign against 62, 63; Evil-Merodach, successor of 89; Jerusalem, burning of Temple in 12, 77, destruction of 77, removal of sacred objects of Temple to Babylonia 68, 92, siege of 74, *75–6* (Ezekiel), 77; Judah, instigates attacks against 63, invasion of 62, 63, *63–5* (Jeremiah), conquest of 12, 77, *77–8* (Lamentations), annexation of part to Samaria 78; Judeans, exile of to Babylonia (in 597) 65, (in 586) 12, 77, (in 582) 78; Saddam Hussein's identification with xii; 'servant' of Yahweh, described as by Jeremiah 70; tribute brought to 16–17n; Tyre, conquest of 81, *82* (Ezekiel)
Nineveh 2, 12, 15, 19, 55, *56–8* (Nahum)

Noph *24* (Hosea), *40* (Isaiah ben Amoz)

Opis 91

Pekah 26
Pekahiah 26
Persia: Assyrian rule of 7; Babylonia, conquest of 89–90, *90–1* (Jeremiah); deportation, reversal of Assyrian-Babylonian policy 6, 91–2, *96–7* (Second Isaiah); idol-worshippers 101; and prophecy 1, 2; Tyre, trade with *83* (Ezekiel); *see also* Cyrus II
Pharaoh Neco 58
Philistia: adjacent to Judah 1, 35; prophecy to, by Isaiah ben Amoz 5, 34, *36*; threat to Israel *29*; wars with Assyria 26, 35, *36* (Isaiah ben Amoz), 46
Phoenicia: Assyria, wars with 26, 33, 45, 46; Isaiah ben Amoz, prophecies to 5, *34–5*, 98; Israel, adjacent to 1, alliance with (9th century) 19; Judah, alliance with (6th century) 77; *see also* Lebanon, Tyre
prophecy, art of: aesthetic pleasure of 105; books of as anthologies 15–16; creative imagination over historical facts, triumph of 1; criticism of 14; exile, threat of and creative flowering of 11; genres, allegory *28* (Isaiah ben Amoz), *66* (Ezekiel), *68–9* (Ezekiel), 73, confession 14, 69, *70–3* (Jeremiah), dirge *27* (Isaiah ben Amoz), *34–5* (Isaiah ben Amoz), *43–4* (Isaiah ben Amoz), *65–6* (Jeremiah), *66–7* (Ezekiel), *81–5* (Ezekiel), lyric 14, 69, *70–3* (Jeremiah), war poetry, see imperialism; and history, related to specific period 1, 5; imperialism, instrument of victory over 1, 105; as 'the most influential body of poetry in history' 14; and iron imagery 8–9, 9–10; 'men speaking to men' 14; and Mesopotamian art, compared with 3–4, 55–6, *Epic of Gilgamesh* 14, lions caged and hunted 14–15,

prophecy—*cont.*
theophany of Ezekiel 74, depiction
of Yahweh and Mesopotamian
kings 3–4, 9–10, 16–17, *46* (Isaiah
ben Amoz), 105, see list of illustrations ix; no parallel elsewhere 1,
5; refrain, use of 27, *28–31* (Isaiah
ben Amoz), 81, *81–5* (Ezekiel)
prophecy, empires and imperialism:
barbarity rarely condemned 3;
influence of upon 1, 100, 105;
inseparability from 8; defence
against and subversion of 1, 4ff., 9–
10, 12, 13, 14, 31, 33, 50–1, 105;
'empire of faith' 50; and kingdom
of God 4; blind to military power
23; misleading picture of in prophets 1–3, 34, 39, 81; monotheism
forced on Judah by 8; 'negation of
empire' 11; victory over 1, 105
prophecy, moral thrust: animals, pro-
hibition of cruelty to *50* (Hosea);
arrogance, opposition to *21* (Amos),
35 (Isaiah ben Amoz), *48* (Isaiah
ben Amoz), *84–5* (Jeremiah); faith,
loss of as cause of Israel's exile
33; injustice of Yahweh 12, 58, *59*
(Jeremiah/Habakkuk); justice,
emphasis upon 5, 14, 20, *21–2*
(Amos), 27, *28–31* (Isaiah ben
Amoz), *33* (Micah), *50* (Hosea), *59*
(Jeremiah/Habakkuk); materialism,
opposition to 14, *21* (Amos); mercy,
Judah's throne is built on mercy 37;
'I will betroth you to me in mercy'
50; moral principles of Yahweh
worship, summed up 31, *32–3*
(Micah); pagan beliefs, invectives
against, *see* idols and idol-worship;
power, opposition to abuse of 14,
21–2 (Amos), *22* (Isaiah ben Amoz);
realpolitik of the spirit 52; religious
integrity, emphasis on in Ezekiel
and Jeremiah 66; sexual licence,
opposition to *21* (Amos), 23; sin,
view that Israel and Judah fell
because of *22* (Amos), 51, *64*
(Jeremiah), *96–7* (Second Isaiah),
exaggeration of 23, punishment of

on Day of Yahweh *54–5*
(Zephaniah), *107–8* (Joel); spirit
rather than letter of the law, emphasis on 14; war and empire, opposition to 11, 20, *50* (Hosea), *104*
(Zechariah); wealth, opposition to
unjust distribution of 14
prophets and prophecy: Assyria,
ambivalence toward 10–12;
appeasement, policy of 47, 66, 70;
authorship, difficult to determine
15; bibliography on 110–11; consolation of *87–8* (Jeremiah/Ezekiel),
95–7 (Second Isaiah); dating,
difficulties in 15, 53; and the 'Day
of the Lord' 50, *54–5* (Zephaniah),
74, *80* (Obadiah), *107–8* (Joel);
defiance 5, *47–8* (Isaiah ben Amoz);
disappearance of 13; earliest writings 20, Ezekiel, only prophet who
prophesied in exile 34; 'false prophets' 16; fragmentation 14, 15–16;
functions of 5, 11, 104–5; God's
injustice, motif of 12, 58, *59*
(Jeremiah/Habakkuk); and guilt
and retribution 5, 50, 51; golden
age predictions 50, 104–5; Hebrew,
quality of 14; importance and
influence of 1, 14; oral tradition of
xi; our ignorance of 16; Isaiah 'a
linguistic match for Assyria's military might' 27; Jerusalem siege
(701), importance in history of 49;
magic, opposition to 11, 13, 14, *39–
40* (Isaiah ben Amoz); Manasseh,
suppression of 53; and messianic
hope 13, *104* (Zechariah), 104–5;
and mythologized history of Israel
31, *32* (Micah); national identity,
attempts to buttress *31–3* (Micah);
optimism of 14, 50–2, 70, 87, *87–
8* (Jeremiah/Ezekiel), *95–7* (Second
Isaiah); personal life symbolic of
nation 23, 70, 74, *75–7* (Ezekiel);
predictions, of return from exile in
Mesopotamia *28* (Hosea), 42, *51*
(Hosea), 87, *88* (Jeremiah),
89 (Ezekiel), 98, of return of
other nations from exile 98, of last

prophets and prophecy—*cont.*
prophets 103–4; resistance, Isaiah's call for *47–8*; violent thrust of 3, 14, *54–5* (Zephaniah), *56–8* (Nahum), *60–1* (Jeremiah), *62–3* (Joel), *63–5* (Jeremiah), *68–9* (Jeremiah), *73* (Jeremiah), *76* (Ezekiel), *81–5* (Ezekiel), *90–1* (Jeremiah), *106* (Habakkuk); waves of, coincident with waves of imperial conquest 4; *see also* under individual prophets, idols and idol-worship, Israel, Judah, Judaism, Mesopotamian inscriptions, Yahweh

Qarkar, battle of (c. 853) 20

Rezin 26, *29*

Samaria (=Shomron, capital of kingdom of Israel) 9, *21–2* (Amos), 23, *28* (Isaiah ben Amoz), 33
Samaria (Assyrian/Babylonian province in the conquered territory of Israel) 33, 78, 98
Sargon II: capture of Samaria (721) 23; death of 10, 45; model of Assyrian conqueror 4; success in consolidating Assyrian empire 7; as 'unwitting saviour of Judah' 8; wars of 34, 39, 42
Scythia 55
Second Isaiah: consolation and return, position of prophecies of in book of *Isaiah* 49–50, *95*; Cyrus II, victories and Edict of Return, reaction to 12–13, *93–5*; idol-worship, vituperative mockery of 10; 'marriage' of Yahweh to Israel *96–7*; Persian empire, leading prophet of 1; 'suffering servant' *99–100*
Sennacherib: death of 10; Isaiah's poem to 15, *47–8*; success in consolidating Assyrian empire 7, 12; as 'unwitting saviour of Judah' 8; wars of 42, 46ff.
Shallum 26
Shalmaneser III: Black Obelisk of 19;

death of 10; model of Assyrian conqueror 4
Shalmaneser V: death of 10; success in consolidating Assyrian empire 7
Sheshbazzar 92
'Song of Deborah' *4*
'Song of Moses' *3–4*

Tanis *40* (Isaiah ben Amoz)
Tarshish *34–5* (Isaiah ben Amoz)
Taurus mountains 7
Tema *38*, 42
Tiglath Pileser III: conquests 5, 7, 19, 26–7, 42; death of 10; as 'unwitting saviour of Judah' 8
Tyre: Assyrian conquest of *34–5* (Isaiah ben Amoz), 74, 81; Babylonian conquest of 74, 81, *81–5* (Ezekiel); trade of *34–5* (Isaiah ben Amoz), *83–4* (Ezekiel); model of tranquility *24* (Hosea)

Urartu 26

war *see* Imperialism and war

Yahweh (=Adonai, Adonai Zebaot, Kedosh Yisrael [Holy One of Israel]): Assyria, 'rod of my wrath' 29; axe of 10; bloodthirsty 3; 'bowman' 9; 'has broken the tyrant's rod' 45; 'chariot-driver' 9; cuckolded husband 31; 'Day of the Lord' 50, *54–5* (Zephaniah), 74, *80* (Obadiah), *107–8* (Joel); empires, use of, to castigate Israel and Judah 2, 10, 12, 20, *29* (Isaiah ben Amoz), 42, 70, to create own spiritual empire 10, 81, *90* (Jeremiah), 105; exile, transformation of by 98; evil, creation of *93* (Second Isaiah); faith in *107* (Habakkuk); father 23, *25–6* (Hosea), 31; fortress *108* (Joel); 'glorious crown of his people' 22; 'God in hiding' 94; God of justice *93–4* (Second Isaiah); God of the nations 20, 94, 104–5; history, determines *48* (Isaiah ben Amoz), *93–4* (Second Isaiah); idols and

Yahweh—*cont.*

idol-worshippers, fury at *3–4* (Song of Moses), *46* (Isaiah ben Amoz), *54–55* (Zephaniah), *72* (Jeremiah), 101, *101–3* (Second Isaiah), advantage over of Yahweh's invisibility 101; injustice of 12, 58, *59* (Jeremiah/Habakkuk), 80; Israel and Judah, fury at 22, *24–25* (Hosea), *29* (Isaiah ben Amoz), *31* (Isaiah ben Amoz), quarrel with *32* (Micah); 'king of the universe' 1; 'king of the whole earth' 4; Israel, abandonment by 27, covenant with 31, demands of *32–3* (Micah), 'marriage' to 23, 31, *50* (Hosea), 95, *96–7* (Second Isaiah), fury at 22, *24–5* (Hosea); Jerusalem, vindication of in siege of (701) 49; 'killer-storm' 22; lion *26* (Hosea), *45* (Isaiah ben Amoz), *51* (Hosea); Master of the Universe 98; and Mesopotamian kings 3–4, 9–10, 16–17, *46* (Isaiah ben Amoz), 105; religious reforms: Hezekiah 45, Josiah 54, 68; 'riding on a cloud' *39* (Isaiah ben Amoz); 'ruthless man of war 71, *105–7* (Habakkuk); saviour of his people *106* (Habakkuk); seducer *70* (Jeremiah); servant of Israel *93* (Second Isaiah), *99–100* (Second Isaiah), Nebuchadrezzar 70; 'shield' 9; smith-creator 9–10; 'ultimate imperial conqueror' 105; vengeful 31, *39–41* (Isaiah ben Amoz), *54–5* (Zephaniah), *60* (Jeremiah), *71* (Jeremiah), *84–5* (Ezekiel), *90–1* (Jeremiah), *105–8* (Habakkuk/Joel); view of by Assyrians 47; vine, planter of *28* (Isaiah ben Amoz); 'wall' 9; warrior *3–4* (Song of Moses), *71* (Jeremiah), *105–7* (Habakkuk); worship of 13, 20, 32, *32–3* (Micah), 45, 54, 98; *see also* idols and idol-worship, Judaism, prophets and prophecy

Zecharia 26
Zechariah 4, *104*
Zedekiah 65, 77
Zephaniah *54–5*
Zerubbabel 93, 104
Zidon *34* (Isaiah ben Amoz)